It's As Easy As ABC

It's As Easy As ABC

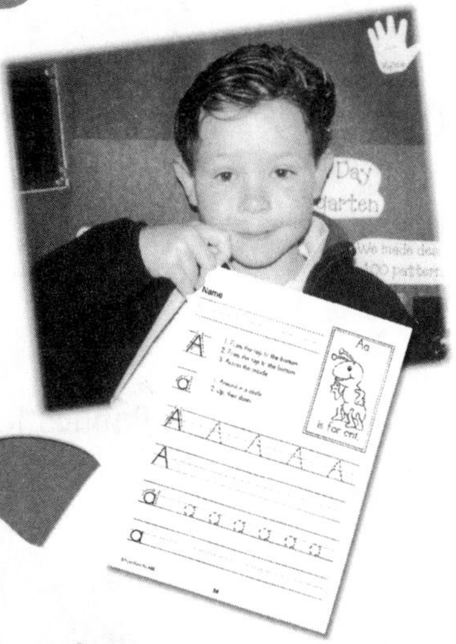

The Essential Elements of a Balanced Literacy Program

by Tracy Jarboe and Stefani Sadler

Crystal Springs BOOKS

A Division of Staff Development for Educators (SDE)

Peterborough, New Hampshire

Published by:

Crystal Springs Books
75 Jaffrey Rd.
PO Box 500
Peterborough, NH 03458
1-800-321-0401
www.crystalsprings.com
www.sde.com

Library of Congress Cataloging-in-Publication Data

Jarboe, Tracy, 1964-
It's as easy as ABC : the essential elements of a balanced literacy program / by Tracy Jarboe and Stefani Sadler ; illustrated by Stefani Sadler.
p. cm.
Includes index.
ISBN 1-884548-46-6 (pbk.)
1. Language arts (Preschool) 2. Language arts (Primary) 3. Early childhood education—Activity programs. I. Sadler, Stefani, 1951- II. Title.
LB1140.5.L3 J37 2002

2002007515

Editor: Meredith A. Reed O'Donnell
Art Director and Production Coordinator: Soosen Dunholter
Illustrator: Stefani Sadler

Dedication

We would like to dedicate this to our parents. Thank you for your patience, love, and encouragement as you continue to lead us through the ABC's of life.

We would also like to dedicate this book to all the young children who have richly blessed our lives through their wonderment and creativity in the learning process. We are thankful for their inspiration, as they are the reason we love teaching.

Preface

As teachers with more than 25 years of combined experience working with young children, we have always found that a balanced approach to our language arts instruction is the most successful framework for developing literacy skills in young children. We identify with and practice the ideologies and instructional techniques of prominent educational leaders like Kenneth Goodman, Don Holdaway, Patricia Cunningham, and Gay Su Pinnell, and we encourage teachers to immerse their students in reading, writing, listening, speaking, illustrating, predicting, observing, experiencing, doing, and creating. Students should be provided with the rich language of fiction, nonfiction, poetry, songs, and chants that span the entire curriculum.

Even though we now have a wealth of quality materials and training available to us, as teachers we are always learning and modifying our educational practices and supplementing the district-adopted curricula. We face the same challenges that you, as educators, face and have, therefore, sought to create a comprehensive book of literacy activities and patterns that will assist you in further promoting readiness and skill development in young children.

The activities and patterns found within *It's As Easy As ABC* are intended to enhance, complement, and extend the concepts already taught within your core literacy instruction. We sincerely hope you and your students find *ABC* stimulating and enjoyable!

Contents

How to Use This Book

It's As Easy As ABC contains patterns and activities designed to supplement core literacy instruction, allowing students to work independently in learning centers, at home, or in class . . . while you're working with small groups! You will find instructions for individual activities at the beginning of each section.

Section 1

The Essential Elements of a Balanced Literacy Program

This first section discusses how to create a balanced literacy program in your classroom. It offers a listing, definition, and implementation of many key instructional elements found within an integrated literacy program.

Section 2

ABC Print with Me: Manuscript Practice Pages for Beginners

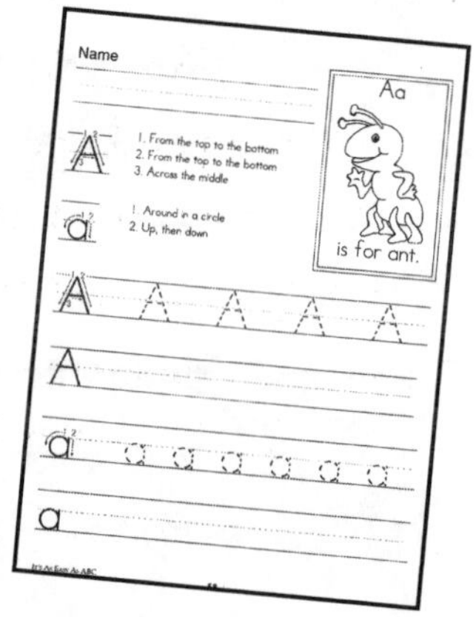

This section is designed to teach correct letter formation and provide manuscript practice with letter/sound picture cues and written instructions.

Section 3

ABC Alphacards: Multipurpose Alphabet Cards with Picture Cues

Alphacards strengthen letter/sound recognition. These patterns may be used on hats or as flash cards, alphabet or coloring books, puppets, alphabet strips, or word-wall labels.

Section 4

ABC Read with Me: Early Emergent Level Books Focusing on Letter/Sound Recognition

These alphabet books strengthen letter/sound recognition, print concepts, and book-handling skills in the early emergent reader.

Section 5

ABC Read with Me: Emergent Level Books Focusing on the Use of High-Frequency Words

These books strengthen vocabulary, high-frequency word recognition, and print concepts in the emergent reader.

Section 6

ABC Rhyme with Me: A–Z Pocket Chart Poetry Activities, Poem Cards, and Student-Made Books

This final section contains activities and a collection of poems (one for each letter of the alphabet), which incorporate rich language, rhyme, and meter. You will also find activities and a book pattern for each poem, designed to extend and enrich learning.

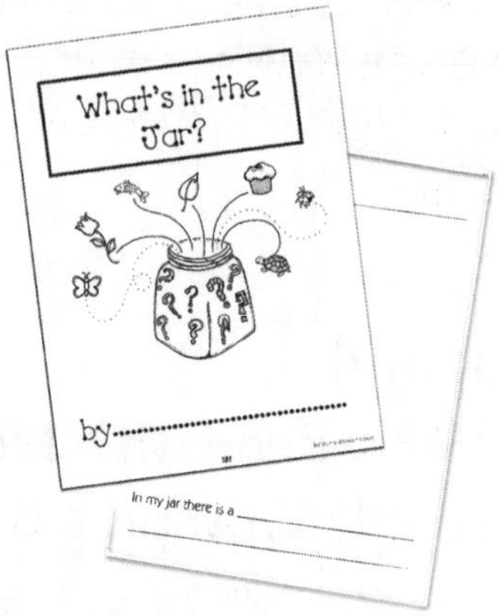

The Essential Elements of a Balanced Literacy Program

We have found it easy and rewarding to incorporate a variety of literacy elements into our day to create a balanced program. We have provided many of these elements on the following pages, and we encourage you to refer to the resource list (pages 34–35) for other informative titles written by many of today's leaders in education.

Your Classroom: A Positive Print-Rich Environment

A print-rich environment stimulates reading and writing. Research and practice have determined that children learn best when they are surrounded by meaningful environmental print: teacher- and student-made labels, signs, charts, poems, songs, books, magazines, newspapers, literacy centers, and word walls. It is in this type of environment that students learn to value reading and writing, in addition to gaining an understanding that both exercises take on many different forms. Of course, books are the most elemental component of a print-rich environment. Numerous books in a variety of genres, levels, and writing styles must be available, readily accessible, and rotated on a regular basis. In other words, do not keep the same 30 titles out all year long. Rotate books by theme, independent reading level, author, and any other category you can think of. Have fun with it!

Children learn best when they are surrounded by meaningful environmental print.

As always, be sure to praise your students for what they attempt to do and ensure that they are not punished for what they cannot do yet. We know that each student is unique and wondrous, entering the classroom with different personal experiences and practice. Some have been read to constantly, propped up in their mothers' laps with a book from the moment they were born, while others may scarcely have had the opportunity to share in a story at all. We all know that as teachers it is our responsibility to provide a positive experience for all our students.

Word of the Day

Skills reinforced with "word of the day" include:

- word and letter sense
- word analysis
- vocabulary development
- syllabication

Each day choose a special word on which to focus. You might consider starting with student names, then high-frequency words, and then, perhaps, special vocabulary words from your literature selections.

- Write each day's word on a sentence strip while discussing the writing.
- Talk about how many letters there are in the word and their shape, sound, and size.
- Cut around this word to highlight its structure.

- Clap the syllables and count the letters in the word.
- See how many other words you can make out of the letters in this special "word of the day."
- Hang it up on your word wall or add it to each student's word bank—a list of words students have mastered that can be placed on a ring, in a folder, or on a poster.

Remember to use the "word of the day" as often as you can, and encourage students to share each time they see it being used. Before you know it, they will be incorporating it correctly into their everyday vocabulary. Have fun! You will be surprised at how many words students will learn by the end of the year.

You will be surprised at how many words students will learn by the end of the year.

Reading/Writing Centers

Teachers know it is important to give students as much opportunity to read and write as possible, but we often express our frustration in trying to manage a classroom *and* provide quality small-group instruction time. A successful solution to this time-management dilemma is the use of classroom reading and writing centers. The key to success is thoughtfully introducing the centers, one at a time, at the beginning of the year, while setting and maintaining high behavioral expectations. If you follow this procedure, the students will impress you with their capabilities and ownership of the learning process. There exists a multitude of learning-center resources on the market; we have included our favorite titles in Instructional Resources, pages 34–35.

Below is a list of center themes, activities, and suggested materials. For assessment purposes, we listed (in parentheses) specific, individual skills and broader skills, topics, and concepts each center or activity reinforces.

PUNCTUATION STATION: Include any activity that involves the use of punctuation. (punctuation)

NAME CENTER: Try any activity that involves the manipulation of student names. Examples include decorating student names, alphabetizing student names, or making student name puzzles, name songs, chants, and poems. (word and letter sense/phonemic awareness)

LIBRARY CORNER: Create a small, cozy space in the classroom filled with books for students to read independently. These books may be library books checked out to the classroom, theme books, class-made books, etc. (print concepts, reading)

LISTENING POST: Create a center in which children are able to listen to books on tape. (print concepts, word analysis, reading fluency, systematic vocabulary development)

POETRY on POCKET CHARTS: Transfer lines from poems, songs, or chants onto sentence strips and watch as students rebuild these (and their own) poems, sliding sentence strips into pocket charts to allow for easy viewing. (word analysis, vocabulary development, punctuation, phonemic awareness, print concepts, text comprehension and analysis)

DAILY SIGN-IN: Each day have students sign in as they enter the classroom. (penmanship)

INVITATIONS: Encourage students to make invitations to classroom functions such as readers theater, poetry readings, etc. (word strategies—graphophonic, semantic, and syntactical cues, dictionaries, word banks, word walls, and environmental print—punctuation, spelling, writing formats)

THANK-YOU NOTES, GET-WELL CARDS, CONGRATULATIONS CARDS: Have students write to one another and classroom guests. (word strategies—graphophonic, semantic, and syntactical cues, dictionaries, word banks, word walls, and environmental print—punctuation, spelling, writing formats)

CLASSROOM MESSAGE BOARD: Use sticky notes, cards, and memos to create a classroom message board. (word strategies, punctuation, spelling)

CLASS-MADE BOOK: Create a class-made book by having each student make his/her own personal page. Bind all the student pages into a large book. Themes might include remakes of a favorite story, innovations, language experience, etc. (print concepts, reading, writing)

STUDENT-MADE BOOKS: Encourage students to make small books of their own. Brainstorm possible topics they can write about and illustrate, or use the student-made book patterns for emergent readers beginning on page 167. (word strategies, print concepts, reading, writing)

POLL MAKING/TAKING: Write a question on a clipboard and have students poll classmates and tally the responses. Later they can share the results with the class. (oral language development, numeration, graphing, analyzing data)

MAGNETIC and TILE LETTER-PLAY: Use various manipulatives to form names, high-frequency words, or vocabulary words. (decoding, word recognition, letter/sound relationships, word analysis)

WORD PUZZLES: Write words on tagboard sentence strips, then cut the letters apart. Students will have fun putting the pieces together to form words. (word and letter sense)

CREATIVE WRITING: Have students write freely and creatively about topics of their own choosing. (word analysis, vocabulary development, punctuation, phonemic awareness, print concepts, text comprehension and analysis)

PHONICS BOARD GAMES: Try word bingo or one of the other word games available on the market, including color word bingo, number word bingo, and high-frequency word bingo. Frank Schaffer, Lakeshore, and Didax are just a few manufacturers that develop these games. (word analysis, vocabulary development)

LETTER MATCHING: Keep letter flash cards on hand for students to match uppercase and lowercase letters. (letter/sound recognition)

LETTER/SOUND RUBBER STAMPS: Kids love stamps! What better way to encourage alphabet and word practice than having students stamp their way to success! Look for alphabet stamps at your local crafts store. (decoding, word recognition, letter/sound relationships, word analysis, alphabetization)

"WORD *from* WORD": Have students make smaller words by using the letters found in larger words. For example, from the word *Thanksgiving,* you can make: *an, in, ant, thank, think, ink, sink, sat,* and so on. This activity is inexhaustible! (decoding, word recognition, letter/sound relationships, word analysis, alphabetization)

SHOPPING LISTS: Children enjoy imitating the adults in their lives. Set up a play home or class store in your room. One of the students' responsibilities when at this home/store is to create shopping lists. This activity helps develop a variety of cross-curricular skills. (phonemic awareness, decoding, word recognition, letter/sound relationships, word analysis, alphabetization, math concepts)

SHAVING CREAM OR PUDDING in TRAYS: You will actually enjoy having your students get their hands messy with this activity! Have them use pudding or shaving cream to practice writing letters and words. Of course, keep some wet wipes on hand to clean those sticky fingers. Using shaving cream has an additional bonus: it cleans the tables and leaves the room smelling great! (phonemic awareness, decoding, word recognition, letter/sound relationships, word analysis, fine-motor skills)

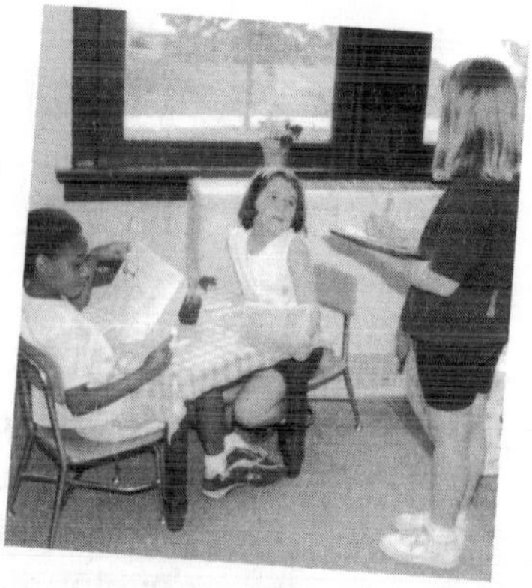

RESTAURANT MENUS: Who doesn't love to eat out, and what child wouldn't have fun taking orders in your very own classroom restaurant. You can create your own menus or ask local eating establishments to donate copies of their menus. (phonemic awareness, decoding, word recognition, letter/sound relationships, word analysis, math concepts)

SCIENCE OBSERVATION JOURNAL: Provide a journal in which students can record their observations at the science center. Their observations might include something about the classroom pet, a garden, or any science concept you and your class are studying. (decoding, word recognition, letter/sound relationships, word analysis, math and science concepts)

BUILDING-BLOCKS JOURNAL: Creativity should be a part of every child's learning. Help students document their creations by encouraging them to design floor plans or a diagram of something they would like to build. Have students consult with fellow classmates, write out their plans, build their creations at the block station, and present them to the class. (decoding, word recognition, letter/sound relationships, word analysis, geometry, graphing)

RHYME PLAY: Rhyming activities abound. Check out your local teachers' supply store, catalog, or game center for rhyming bingo, puppets, and poetry activities. (phonemic awareness, decoding, word recognition, letter/sound relationships, word analysis)

LITE-BRITE: Students will have fun practicing high-frequency words, vocabulary, and even their own names on this favorite toy. (phonemic awareness, decoding, word recognition, letter/sound relationships, word analysis, fine-motor skills)

PLAYDOUGH: Using alphabet cutters, students can cut out words with this favorite malleable manipulative. (phonemic awareness, decoding and word recognition, letter/sound relationships, word analysis, fine-motor skills)

WHITEBOARDS and CHALKBOARDS: The old standbys! You can use these writing spaces for a variety of individual and class-related activities. (phonemic awareness, decoding, word recognition, letter/sound relationships, word analysis, fine-motor skills, punctuation, alphabetization)

Do You See What I See? Do You Hear What I Hear?

Connecting Sight and Sound with Confidence

Dictation

Dictation can't be beat when it comes to giving children individual attention, building fluency in speech, and strengthening confidence in storytelling. Taking dictation is often difficult for the teacher, however, especially with a class of 30 or more students, and you will need to develop ways to spread this exercise out over the course of the day or week. Enlist the help of parents, aides, or cross-age buddies. Few activities develop oral-communication, storytelling, and sequencing skills the way dictation can.

Here's how this exercise works:

1. Preparing: Each child needs a dictation book. Some teachers prefer to create their books using 8½" x 11" plain white paper, which allows space for illustrations, while others prefer to fold the paper in half into an 8½" x 5½" section. Use a three-hole binder, folder, or construction paper cover to protect the book and allow for expansion as the year progresses.

2. Getting Started: Let your students know this book is very special and just for them (for example, they might label it "My Storybook"), something they can use to make up a story using their imaginations. The story can be about *anything* they want. Explain that, when they are ready, you (or a volunteer) will write down the words to their stories and they can work on illustrations.

3. Taking Dictation: When a student brings her/his book to you, say: "Tell me your story" or "How does your story start?" Write down *exactly* what s/he tells you. In order to help a student better formulate her/his story, on occasion read aloud to her/him what s/he has written up to that point. As the year progresses, you can ask students to elaborate, use descriptive words, and work on the concept of beginning, middle, and end.

Few activities develop oral-communication, storytelling, and sequencing skills the way dictation can.

This exercise is a wonderful way to document oral-language growth throughout the year. But don't be disappointed if some children say, "I don't have a story," or if some present you with a hodgepodge of fragmented sentences and ideas. Because these students may not understand the concept of what a story actually is yet, share aloud some of the stories that have been completed successfully—stories students have dictated to a teacher or volunteer—with the entire class. Dictated stories may also be kept in a journal or a dictation log or placed on art. This not only demonstrates the concept of story, it also allows students to feel good about the process.

Talk about student pieces and tales found in books, and explain that authors get their ideas for writing from the stories they have in their *own* heads, just like the students. And be sure to share recollections of your life experiences. This type of modeling develops confidence, trust, and knowledge.

Phonemic Awareness

Current research has shown that phonemic awareness—the awareness that phonemes (see examples in the following songs) are abstractable and manipulative components of the spoken language—is a key predictor of future reading success. When students understand this important concept, they will have the ability to attend to and manipulate the smallest units of the spoken language.

Of course, the more often young children are encouraged to manipulate sounds, the more confidence and success they will have in reading. Focusing on different sizes of linguistic units such as rhyme, syllable, onset-rime (e.g., onset *c* + rime *at*=cat), and phoneme can stimulate phonemic awareness. You can achieve this with your students through the use of sound isolation, blending, segmenting, deleting, and substitution activities (Yopp 1996). Take a look at these fun and instructional song activities below.

> Current research has shown that phonemic awareness is a key predictor of future reading success.

Songs and Rhymes That Strengthen Phonemic Awareness

Song/Rhyme Notes:

- Sing the phoneme's sound—not the letter's name. The same procedure is true for all the letter/sounds represented in the rhymes below.
- At the end of each letter/sound song, sing, to the tune of "Old MacDonald" (and clap, where indicated), the following:

"You all did great, so clap your hands!"
(clap, clap, clap, clap, clap)

Sound Matching (Yopp 1992)
Sing to: *Jimmy Crack Corn and I Don't Care*

> Who has a /d/ word to share with us?
> Who has a /d/ word to share with us?
> Who has a /d/ word to share with us?
> It must start with the /d/ sound!

Individual children volunteer words that begin with the /d/ sound and sing the following:

> *Dog* is a word that starts with /d/.
> *Dog* is a word that starts with /d/.
> *Dog* is a word that starts with /d/.
> *Dog* starts with the /d/ sound!

Sound Isolation (Yopp 1992)
Sing to: *Old MacDonald Had a Farm*

> What's the sound that starts these words:
> *Turtle, time,* and *teeth*?

(* Wait for a response from your students.)

> /T/ is the sound that starts these words:
> *Turtle, time,* and *teeth.*

> With a /t/ /t/ here, and a /t/ /t/ there,
> Here a /t/, there a /t/, everywhere a /t/ /t/.
> /T/ is the sound that starts these words:
> *Turtle, time,* and *teeth.*

> What's the sound in the middle of these words:
> *Leaf* and *deep* and *meat*?
> /Ē/ is the sound in the middle of these words:
> *Leaf* and *deep* and *meat.*

> With an /ē/ /ē/ here, and an /ē/ /ē/ there,
> Here an /ē/, there an /ē/, everywhere an /ē/ /ē/.
> /Ē/ is the sound in the middle of these words:
> *Leaf* and *deep* and *meat.*

> What's the sound at the end of these words:
> *Duck* and *cake* and *beak*?
> /K/ is the sound at the end of these words:
> *Duck* and *cake* and *beak.*

> With a /k/ /k/ here, and a /k/ /k/ there.
> Here a /k/, there a /k/, everywhere a /k/ /k/.
> /K/ is a sound at the end of these words:
> *Duck* and *cake* and *beak.*

Sound Blending (Yopp 1992)
Sing to: *If You're Happy and You Know It*

- Once you have sung once through the verse below, you (the teacher) say a segmented word, such as: /h/ - /a/ - /t/. Students should respond by saying the blended word: hat!

If you think you know this word, shout it out!
If you think you know this word, shout it out!
If you think you know this word,
Then tell me what you heard,
If you think you know this word, shout it out!

Teacher: /h/-/a/-/t/. Students: hat!

Sound Addition or Substitution (Yopp 1992)
Sing to: *Someone's in the Kitchen with Dinah*

- Sound substitutions: *Fe-fi-fiddly-i-o* can become *Be-bi-biddly-i-o* or *Te-ti-tiddly-i-o*, and so on. You can also insert consonant sounds, blends, or diphthongs.

I have a song that we can sing.
I have a song that we can sing.
I have a song that we can sing.
It goes something like this:
Fe-Fi-Fiddly-i-o
Fe-Fi-Fiddly-i-o-o-o-o
Fe-Fi-Fiddly-i-ooooo
Now try it with the /z/ sound!

Ze-Zi-Ziddly-i-o
Ze-Zi-Ziddly-i-o-o-o-o
Ze-Zi-Ziddly-i-ooooo
Now try it with the /ch/ sound!

Note: Substitutions may also be done with the *Ee-igh, ee-igh, oh!* section of the "Old MacDonald" song. For example: *Bee-bigh, bee-bigh, boh!* or *See-sigh, see-sigh, soh!* Sounds can be substituted in many children's songs. The "Happy Birthday" song can be sung: *Bappy Birthday bo boo* instead of "Happy Birthday to you." Or you could sing a particular syllable through the whole song: *Pa-pa Papa pa pa*; or use *la, te, le, lo*, etc. Select a "sound of the day," such as /t/, then say all the children's names with that sound as you call attendance. For example, Billy will be called "Tilly" and Jennifer will be called "Tennifer." Just try to have fun and be creative!

Sound Segmentation (Yopp 1992)
Sing to: *Twinkle, Twinkle, Little Star*

Listen, listen to my word,
Then tell me all the sounds you heard:
Race (*say this slowly).
/R/ is one sound,
/A/ is two,
/S/ is the last in *race*, it's true.

Thanks for listening to my word
And telling me the sounds you heard!

Note: Segmenting sounds in a word is one of the more difficult activities to perform, yet it is highly related to later success in decoding words (Yopp 1992). Segmenting sounds includes the isolation of sounds in words. To begin the segmenting process, the children can play with the isolation of just the first sound in a word. Many popular songs can be modified to include iterations: *P-p-p-p-pop goes the weasel!* Use iteration of children's names too: *H-H-H-H-Heather* or *J-J-J-J-Josh.* Or draw out the sound in an exaggerated manner: *Mmmmmary* or *Sssssssam.*

Reading

Modeled Reading: The Read-Aloud

Read-aloud is a type of modeled reading when you or your team teacher, assistant, or volunteers read books to the students. The books are above the students' instructional levels and are often centered on a teaching theme. Daily read-aloud times are important, as students need to see teachers model the reading process; hear words and sounds, rhythms and patterns, vocal intonations and inflections; and simply enjoy quality literature. This process allows children to experience more complex language structures, story lines, and character development. The class discussions that follow a read-aloud provide an opportunity for students to access higher levels of critical thinking skills.

Daily read-aloud times are important, as students need to see teachers model the reading process; hear words and sounds, rhythms and patterns, vocal intonations and inflections; and simply enjoy quality literature.

Shared Reading

This important and effective element of a balanced reading program was first developed by Don Holdaway to create enjoyable, successful reading experiences using materials *above* a child's independent reading level.

Shared reading differs from modeled reading in that it takes place over several days as the teacher reads a shared text to her/his students (small-group or whole-class), who join in and read along. This process allows students to read material they would not be able to read independently, in a nonthreatening, supportive environment.

Shared reading promotes risk-taking, as the teacher withholds from verbally correcting students' individual mistakes during a unison reading activity. The teacher is able to model the use of print concepts and strategies for predicting, confirming predictions, and self-correcting, while simultaneously teaching skills (e.g., letter/sound, blend, rhyme, punctuation, story structure) in the context of a familiar story.

A shared reading book typically

- is large in size.
- is predictable.
- contains pictures that support the print.
- contains text that has rhyme, rhythm, and repetition.
- is inviting, enjoyable, and easy to remember.
- promotes students' active involvement through movement and drama.
- lends itself to class remakes, innovations, and learning extensions. Ideally, the story should integrate with the current thematic curriculum.

Many teachers use one shared reading book over the course of an instructional week in the following manner:

Day 1. Read the story to your class, pausing occasionally to allow students opportunities to make predictions, and ask open-ended questions such as: *What is this story going to be about? What is on the cover? How did this story make you feel? Who was in the story?* Help develop one-to-one correspondence and directionality in emergent readers by pointing to each word as you read it. The children love to use thematic pointers to make this process even more engaging and fun.

Day 2. Echo- or choral-read the selected book with your students. Try reading the text with an accent, singing it, or using hand movements to dramatize the story. Clap the rhythm as you read. Use the cloze technique by pausing before predictable words or phrases, allowing students to orally fill them in. The students are now becoming actively engaged in their reading.

Day 3. When reading with students, focus on a selected teaching point. Reinforce basic concepts of print such as one-to-one correspondence, directionality, return sweep, and punctuation. Highlighting tape and Wikki Stix are wonderful tools for isolating desired print.

Day 4. Focus on story comprehension, using puppets, hats, and other props to dramatize the story. Match words written on sentence strips to words found in the text. Focus on the vocabulary development by adding words from the story to your word wall or word bank.

Day 5. Create a class innovation (e.g., class-made book) or remake of the story (many teachers prefer to create the story outline in a whole-group setting using sticky notes or chart paper), then place the text on each page using personal manuscript or computer-generated script, and assign one student or groups of students a page to illustrate. When students have completed their story page, bind all the pages together and place this class-made book in your library area so the class may revisit it often.

Guided-Process Reading

We recommend for guided-process reading that you divide students into small, homogeneous groups and use books at each group's instructional level (90 percent accuracy). Do not read these books to the students, but after a quick "picture walk" (to incite interest) guide the students to process the print using a balanced cueing system:

- **Semantic** (Does it *make sense*?). Semantic cues come from a child's life experience.
- **Syntactic** (Does it *sound* right?). Syntactic cues come from knowing how oral language is put together.
- **Graphophonic** (Does it *look* right?). Graphophonic cues come from knowing the relationship between oral language and its graphic symbols (i.e., any letter or character used to represent spoken language).

Do not pre-teach the words, but guide the students to use and develop reading strategies for learning these words on their own. Now, invite students to talk about the story they have read, or suggest they read it again with a buddy. You will know that the reading has been successful if your observations or running records show that students are accessing the different cueing systems and using cross-checking strategies as they read.

Independent Reading

It is essential to set aside time during the day to allow children to independently choose and read books.

Materials for this may include:

- books that are at the students' independent level
- teacher-made books
- class-made books
- familiar books from guided reading and shared reading
- familiar songs, poems, or chant charts

Many teachers refer to independent reading time as DEAR (Drop Everything and Read), SSR (Sustained Silent Reading), or RTR (Read the Room).

WRITING

Student Writing

How do children learn how to write? They learn to write by writing! And you can begin the writing process with your students as soon as school begins. (Keep in mind that writing at this level may take many forms, depending on each child's level of readiness.) We recommend students write every day through activities such as journal writing, guided-process writing, and writers workshop. Encourage your class to use phonetic spelling, and provide them with plain unlined paper when they first begin to write. Putting pencil to paper can be an overwhelming experience for young writers to begin with. Actually writing on a line may be too much of a challenge and further intimidate them. Introduce lined paper as students demonstrate readiness.

How do children learn how to write?
They learn to write by writing!

Phonetic Spelling

The term *phonetic spelling* can be defined as writing the sounds you hear, in the order you hear them. Stretching out words and saying them slowly enhances the process. To provide students with a visual representation, try slowly stretching apart a rubber band as you verbally stretch out the word. You might also try using the following procedure, first introduced to us by national language-arts specialist Anne Diskin.

Hold up a dictionary and ask your students if they know what it is: *"A dictionary.* You are right! What do we look for in a dictionary? *Words.* You are right again! There are hundreds and thousands of words in a dictionary. Do you know that I have been in school for __ years. That's an enormous amount of learning time, and I have not learned all these words yet. How many years have you been in school? Well, no one expects you to be able to spell all these words, either. You and I have many more words in our heads than we know how to spell."

Here's how a sample lesson might look and sound:

"Let's write the word *alligator*. If I want to write this word and I am not sure how to spell it, I will have to make a choice. I can:

Draw a picture of an *alligator*.

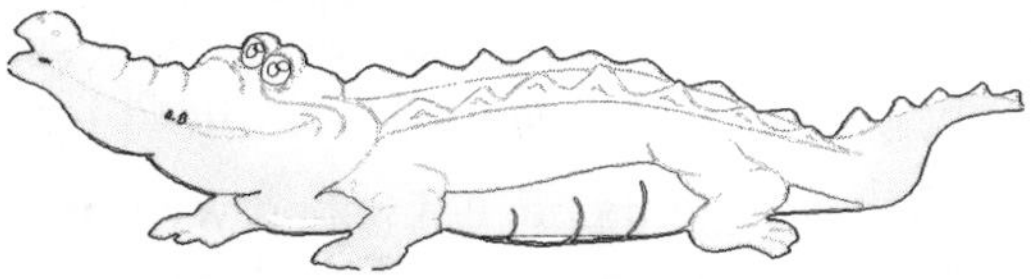

Pretend to spell the word *alligator;* spell it like this: 

"Is that long enough? (Wait for students' responses.) Let's stretch the word out: *al - li - ga - tor*. No! I need to write it like this:

"Now I'll try phonetic spelling and attempt to guess the letters by listening to the sounds. So when we say *alligator,* what sound do we hear at the beginning? What letter do you think makes that sound? So a phonetic spelling might look like this:

"What sound do you hear at the end of the word? (Ask students to respond.) Yes, those are good answers. We do hear an /r/, so an estimated spelling can look like this too:

"Do you hear the sounds in the middle of the word? What letters do you hear? Good listening! So phonetic spelling can look like this too: *aligtr.*

"These are all ways to write a word when you are not sure how it is spelled in the dictionary. Let's try to spell some words together."

You may give phonetic spelling tests to encourage children to simply write words (this will also help build their confidence). Here's how you might introduce the test:

1. Give out blank sheets of paper and say, "Now you are able to write any word you want by either drawing, pretending to write, or using phonetic spelling. I'm going to say some words, which I would like you to write down on your paper. Everything that you write will be correct!"

2. Call out some words like *cat*, *dog*, *mom*, and *dad*, and walk around the room, giving lots of praise: "Super phonetic spelling!" or "Gosh, you are an excellent writer!" Remember that students' writings may be in pictorial form, and that is okay. Work through this process on a daily basis until each child is comfortable writing at his/her level (this process could take several weeks), at which point you can incorporate more writing activities into your day without fears or tears.

3. Once students have finished writing, write the words below *their* spellings, using the correct conventional spelling. If you are worried about hurting their feelings or taking away from their efforts, here is a good way to explain it: "Your parent(s) (or guardians/the adult figure(s) in their homes) need a translation, because they do not have the ability to read phonetic spelling like we do. Because of this we will need to write a bilingual book. Your phonetic spelling will be on the top and my 'book spelling' will be underneath." Ask students to read back the book spelling you have modeled. This process allows children to transition from phonetic spelling to conventional spelling.

Try as often as possible to model the correct spelling beneath students' writing, remembering to talk about the various writing conventions: capitalization, punctuation, spacing, and spelling. Do not make every corrected mistake a teaching point, as children at this age will have many, and correcting them all would result in confusion and frustration. Choose one or two teaching points on which to focus, and spend time developing these. By your choosing one or two teaching points, the child is able to focus on that concept and you can transfer the learning successfully. When you get to those tricky spellings that make no phonetic sense, such as *are, the, their*, etc., have the student shout, "That doesn't make sense!"or "That's ridiculous!" This allows her/him to feel even more comfortable with her/his attempts at writing. Remember to praise all efforts and have fun!

Do not make every corrected mistake a teaching point. Choose one or two teaching points on which to focus, and spend time developing these.

Modeled Writing

Modeled writing allows for students to watch the teacher write as s/he demonstrates different components of the writing process and talks about the conventions of print, such as left-to-right directionality, spacing between words, etc. Students can actively participate in the content of the writing while the teacher interacts with them about sentence structure, letters, and punctuation. The defining element is that you, as the teacher, control the pen.

Daily News

A popular form of modeled writing in the classroom is the daily news, which, in addition to the calendar, many teachers begin or end their days with. After you have decided which time works best for you, try projecting modeled writing pieces using an overhead projector, as it is easy to write on and large enough for all the children to see. Make a copy of the transparency to place in a class book. Children enjoy reading this collaborative model, which becomes a record of class learning and special events. If you do not use an overhead projector, try using chart paper or a whiteboard.

The key to presenting the daily news is modeling. Talk and think out loud as you write, sometimes pausing and sometimes voicing your thoughts to your students. Don't be afraid to cross things out if you change your mind or make a mistake; it is actually very important that you let your students watch you work through this exercise, voicing your thought process and editing text.

Here's an example:

> Today is ~~Janury~~ January 31, 2002. It is the
> last day of the month. We are going to ~~a~~ an assembly
> this ~~morning~~ afternoon at one o'clock. Anne said,
> "Tomorrow is ~~me's~~ my birthday!"

We recommend you keep the news very brief at the beginning of the year (5 to 10 minutes), but it can increase in length and complexity as the year progresses. Model the news at first, but later in the year allow it to become an interactive exercise. If you have a VIP or "star of the day," for example, this student can add some personal news. Be sure to include her or his name, e.g., Scott said, "I'm going to Pizza Hut with my mom after school."

If you have a group of limited English proficient students or a group of kinesthetic learners, you may want to add physical movements, such as those listed below, to the news when you read it aloud. Try out these ideas when you're reading to students. (*Note*: Start with one movement at a time and add progressively.)

- March in place while reading (emphasize the rhythm of the syllables).
- Hold your arms high in the air for each capital letter.
- Place your hands out in a stop position each time you come to a period.

- Jump each time you come to a comma.
- Make quotation marks with your fingers when you see them.
- Put your hand on your chin as if you are thinking, or scratch your head, when you see a question mark.
- Put your hands high in the air and shake them when you see an exclamation mark.

Interactive Writing

Interactive writing is a teaching method that helps young children learn how to read and write in a large- or small-group setting. Unlike modeled writing, during the interactive writing process you share the pen with your students. The students decide what will be written, and the teacher acts as a guide/facilitator. Together, say the sentence and count the number of words (a pre-writing activity), then begin to write.

Ask the students what the first sound in the first word is in the text you and your students have determined together. Ask if someone knows how to form the letter that makes the sound that starts the word, then invite that student up to the writing surface you are using (e.g., chart paper, whiteboard, etc.) to begin the writing process. Stretch the word out slowly. When the student comes to a tricky letter, you may take ownership of the pen and write that letter or word.

Before actually allowing the student to write, however, make sure s/he has guessed the letter correctly. If a student has made an incorrect guess, praise her/his attempt and ask if another student can help. The first student remains in control of the pen during this collaborative effort. If a mistake is made, have her/him put a line through it, or better yet, cover it with a piece of white sticky tape, which s/he can write over. Encourage children to begin writing chunks of words and eventually entire words and sentences. Each time you complete a word, reread the sentence together. This facilitates cross-checking strategies and strengthens reading. After you have finished writing, leave the writing out for students to revisit while "reading" the room.

Guided-Process Writing (GPW)

Guided-process writing follows guided-process reading in our classroom, and it immediately allows students to make connections between reading and writing.

GPW allows students to make connections between reading and writing.

In guided-process writing the teacher guides students through the writing process as the children make sense of the print. We strongly recommend you work in small groups, allowing for one-on-one interactions with each student at her/his instructional level, encouraging her/him to write what s/he knows and to focus on letter/sound connections. You can model what is unknown by deciding to focus on a specific teaching point or object for each lesson, while reinforcing and guiding approximations along the way.

GPW Books

Make a GPW book for each student by taking 15 sheets of 8½" x 11" white paper and one sheet of 8½" x 11" colored construction paper, folding them in half width-wise, and stapling them together along the "spine," remembering to place the construction paper on the outside to form a cover. (If you want to make a binder of student work, you can three-hole-punch 8½" x 11" papers instead.) When students open up their books, they will write on the bottom portion, and you will write on the top portion. If you prefer the 8½" x 11" format, you could simply draw a line across the middle of a sheet of white paper, using the top section for your writing.

Discuss the book you read during GPR time and ask each student to write about this book in her/his own GPW book. For example, let's say you have just finished reading a book called "In the Classroom," in which the text follows a predictable pattern, starting with: "I saw a pencil (other objects/people follow—e.g., *I saw a teacher. I saw a whiteboard,* etc.). Encourage students to write what else they see in a classroom using a similar sentence pattern: "I saw a _____ (name of object)." Make sure students have enough time to think about what they would like to write.

This is a great "teachable moment" time to circulate and meet one-on-one with each student in the group, helping her/him with the writing process and making select teaching points.

When you are demonstrating a teaching point, e.g., spelling, capitalization, or punctuation, your writing is always on the top portion of the paper, and the student makes the corrections to her/his writing below. Remember that students should only be expected to produce writing that is semantically, syntactically, and graphophonically appropriate for their developmental levels. This is a wonderful time to incorporate writing tools such as high-frequency word lists, word walls, and sound cards.

Writers Workshop

Writers Workshop incorporates three steps at the early emergent level: pre-writing, writing, and sharing.

PRE-WRITING may include reading a story, poem, or song, or holding a discussion about a piece of literature that helps prepare students for writing time. During pre-writing, access prior knowledge by asking questions about the story topic (this allows students to attach personal experience to the subject matter) and brainstorm writing topics. You may even wish to demonstrate writing at this time through creating a story map or alternate endings or by identifying key words.

WRITING may take the form of drawing for many kindergarteners. For some students, writing may actually have nothing to do with the pre-writing activity, as young children are known for their ability to wander off topic and be creative.You could teach a spectacular lesson on the life cycle of a plant but discover students writing about rainbows, unicorns, or their uncle Fred's big truck, and that's okay. The focus in beginning writing instruction is to simply have students put pencil to paper and understand that thoughts can take written form. Right now, children just need some form of a story starter to build their confidence and get them on task. The focus may change as students develop confidence and ability, and at that point you may start to focus on such issues as attention to task and topic; creating a beginning, middle, and end; character development; and so on.

SHARING usually means coming together as a group and giving some children an opportunity to "read" what they have written. Some classrooms have an "Authors Corner" or "Authors Chair" in or around which the class can gather and listen to the student-author. This same process can be used during your journal time. With first grade students, include additional steps such as editing, revising, and publishing.

PARENT-HOME CONNECTION

Parents (students, too) need to know what the learning expectations are for their children, what current educational research states, and what your teaching practices are. Many schools provide the chance to share such information at an orientation, back-to-school, or curriculum night. Explain to parents what terms like *phonemic awareness, phonics, phonetic writing, guided reading, literature-based,* and *reading stages* mean. Let parents know about great books like *Writing Begins at Home* by Marie Clay and *Raising Lifelong Learners* by Lucy Calkins. Consider having these books and others available for parents to review.

Teachers, you have the opportunity to empower parents to effectively and positively reinforce and expand on classroom learning at home. Hosting special family nights ("Family Literacy Night," for example), during which you model curriculum and instructional methods, can help open the communication lines with your most important supporters. During such a night, invite parents and students to join you in participating in activities you have carefully designed and modeled. Parents are able to see and practice instructional techniques, which they can use again at home while working with their children.

The key to creating a successful learning partnership is to get parents involved, excited, and empowered! One fun activity for students and their parents to work on is a collaborative-writing piece, in which you write a question in a home-school journal (e.g., "What do you remember about kindergarten?"), to which parents and students respond. Another good activity is the classic "every child takes home the class stuffed animal or pet and writes about its adventures." To further develop this concept, you might be interested in purchasing a title from the variety of collaborative homework resources available through educational resource catalogs.

The key to creating a successful learning partnership is to get parents involved, excited, and empowered!

Instructional Resources

. . . And with a Light Touch: Learning About Reading, Writing, and Teaching with First Graders
- Carol Avery (Heinemann)

Buddy Reading: Cross-Age Tutoring in a Multicultural School
- Katharine Davies Samway, Gail Whang, and Mary Pippit (Heinemann)

Classroom Experiences: The Writing Process in Action
- Naomi Gordon (Heinemann)

Classroom Routines That Really Work for Pre-K and Kindergarten
- Kathleen Hayes and Renee Creange (Scholastic)

Classrooms That Work: They Can All Read and Write
- Patricia M. Cunningham (Addison-Wesley/Longman)

Endangered Minds: Why Children Don't Think—And What We Can Do About It
- Jane M. Healy (Touchstone Books)

The Energy to Teach
- Donald Graves (Heinemann)

Evaluating Literacy: A Perspective for Change
- Robert J. Anthony, Alison Preece, Terry D. Johnson, and Norma Mickelson (Heinemann)

The Foundations of Literacy
- Don Holdaway (Heinemann)

Guided Reading: Good First Reading for All Children
- Irene C. Fountas and Gay Su Pinnell (Heinemann)

Hey! I Can Read This! The Interactive Book Experience
- Donna Butt and Kathy Thurman (Crystal Springs Books)

Interactive Writing: How Language and Literacy Come Together
- Andrea McCarrier, Gay Su Pinnell, and Irene C. Fountas (Heinemann)

Invitations: Changing As Teachers and Learners
- Regie Routman (Heinemann)

Joyful Learning in Kindergarten
- Bobbi Fisher (Heinemann)

Kids Have All the Write Stuff
- Sharon A. Edwards and Robert W. Maloy (Penguin)

Lasting Impressions: Weaving Literature into the Writing Workshop
- Shelley Harwayne (Heinemann)

Literacy at the Crossroads: Crucial Talk About Reading, Writing, and Other Teaching Dilemmas
- Regie Routman (Heinemann)

Literacy Instruction in Half- and Whole-Day Kindergarten
- Lesley Mandel Morrow, Dorothy S. Strickland, and Deborah Gee Woo (IRA)

Literature Based Reading Activities
- Ruth Hellen Yopp and Hallie K. Yopp (Allyn & Bacon/Longman)

Making Big Words
- Patricia M. Cunningham (Good Apple)

Making Standards Work: How to Implement Standards-Based Assessments in the Classroom, School, and District
- Douglas B. Reeves (Advanced Learning Centers)

Making Words
- Patricia M. Cunningham (Good Apple)

Matching Books to Readers: Using Leveled Books in Guided Reading (K–3)
- Irene C. Fountas and Gay Su Pinnell (Heinemann)

Month by Month Reading and Writing for Kindergarten
- Patricia M. Cunningham and Dorothy P. Hall (Carson Dellosa)

On Solid Ground: Strategies for Teaching Reading, K–3
- Sharon Taberski (Heinemann)

Phonics They Use
- Patricia M. Cunningham (Addison Wesley)

Raising Lifelong Learners: A Parents Guide
- Lucy M. Calkins (Perseus Press)

The Scholastic Big Book of Word Walls
- Mary Beth Spann (Scholastic)

Spel . . . . Is a Four Letter Word
- J. Richard Gentry (Heinemann)

Spelling Through Phonics
- Marlene J. McCracken and Robert A. McCracken (Peguis Publishers)

Towards a Reading-Writing Classroom
- Andrea Butler and Jan Turbill (Heinemann)

26 Easy and Adorable Alphabet Recipes for Snacktime
- Tracy Jarboe and Stefani Sadler (Scholastic)

What Are the Other Kids Doing . . . While You Teach Groups
- Donna Marriott (Creative Teaching Press)

Word Matters: Teaching Phonics and Spelling in the Reading/Writing Classroom
- Irene C. Fountas and Gay Su Pinnell (Heinemann)

Words Their Way: Word Study for Phonics, Vocabulary, and Spelling Instruction
- Donald R. Bear, Marcia Invernizzi, Francine Johnston (Prentice Hall)

Writing Begins at Home: Preparing Children for Writing Before They Go to School
- Marie M. Clay (Heinemann)

Scheduling Instruction: Getting It All In

A prerequisite for the formation of an instructional schedule is FLEXIBILITY! While there is no one perfect schedule, every schedule needs to be adaptable. We have included our own scheduling options below for you to consider.

Half-Day Kindergarten

8:00 a.m.	Opening/Roll/Flag/Calendar/Daily News/Word of the Day
8:30	Shared Reading and Shared Writing: Big Book and Poetry
9:00	Rotations: GPR/Phonics/Journal/Writers Workshop
10:00	Recess/Nutrition
10:15	Math
10:45	Art/Social Studies/Science/Centers
11:15	Close
11:30	Dismissal

Extended-Day Kindergarten

8:00 a.m.	Opening/Roll/Flag/Calendar
8:30	Word Play
9:00	Shared Reading and Writing
9:45	Recess
10:00	GPR and GPW/Phonics/Journal/Writers Workshop
11:30	Lunch
12:00 p.m.	Read-Aloud or Silent Reading
12:15	Math
1:00	Social Studies/Science/Art/Centers
1:45	Close/Daily News
2:00	Dismissal

First Grade

8:00 a.m.	Opening/Roll/Calendar/Flag
8:30	Word Study/Phonics/Vocabulary/Spelling
9:00	Shared Reading, Writing, and Poetry
9:30	Recess
9:45	GPR and GPW/Seat-work/Journals/Centers
11:15	Lunch
11:45	Read-Aloud
12:00 p.m.	Math/Centers
1:00	PE
1:15	Writers Workshop/Integrated Language Arts
1:50	Closing
2:00	Dismissal

Section 2

ABC Print with Me: Manuscript Practice Pages for Beginners

The following printing practice pages have been designed with both verbal and visual cues to assist your students in learning. The correct formation of each letter is clearly defined and easy to follow. We have provided a picture and a word that begin with each focus letter in order to assist in the process of letter/sound relationship and acquisition, but we strongly urge you to review directions on how to form each letter with your class according to the numbered steps we have provided.

Start by having students put their pencils to their papers and read the directions, while you visually demonstrate how each letter is formed.

Let's take a look at the directions for capital *A*. You might say:

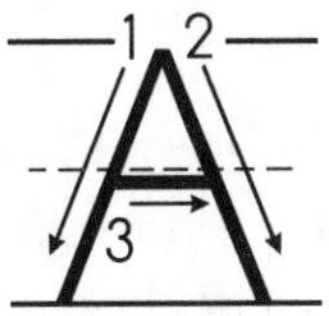

"Everyone place his/her pencil tip on the top of the writing line. Now, (1) draw a line (at a slight angle) from the top to the bottom. Pick your pencil point up and place it on the top of the manuscript line where you started your first line. Now, (2) draw a new line (at a slight angle) from the top to the bottom. Pick your point up one more time and (3) draw a line across the middle."

Note: "From the *top* to the *bottom*": *top* and *bottom* refer to the top and bottom of the manuscript writing line.

"Across the *middle*": *middle* refers to the dotted line that marks the middle of the manuscript writing line.

Activities for Manuscript Practice Pages

Once students have completed a manuscript practice page for each letter of the alphabet, try one or more of the following activities-great for small groups or learning centers.

Take-Home Books: Combine individual student pages (manuscript practice pages A-Z) into a take-home book for each student.

In-Class Books: Divide practice pages by individual letters and bind them into 26 books to keep in the classroom. Do this once at the beginning/middle of the school year and again at the end. Students will enjoy seeing how their handwriting has improved! (If you want to make pages anonymous, simply cover student names with white Post-it Tape, then photocopy.)

Homework: Photocopy and bind pages A-Z into a manuscript practice homework book for each student to complete with his/her parents. The illustrations and written cues make this the perfect homework activity.

Games: Make the pictures that correspond to each letter of the alphabet into alphabet picture cards (picture boxes appear in the upper right-hand corner of each manuscript practice page). To make uppercase and lowercase alphabet picture cards, simply photocopy manuscript practice pages, covering the capital letters with removable Post-it Tape. Photocopy again, this time covering the lowercase letter. Cut each picture card box out, color, and laminate. Note: The Alphacards found in Section 3 also work well for the alphabetical order and memory game activities listed. Just cover the capital letter on each card with removable Post-it Tape. Photocopy. Photocopy again, but this time cover the lowercase letter on each card and allow the capital letter to remain visible. Now you should have a complete set of capital letter cards and a complete set of lowercase letter cards. Color, laminate, and trim each card.

- Alphabetical Order: Shuffle the A-Z capital or lowercase cards. Have students place the cards in alphabetical order.

- Memory Game: Shuffle the cards and place them face down in a square grid on the floor. Each player takes a turn flipping two cards over at once. If the player matches an uppercase letter half with its lowercase counterpart, s/he picks both cards up and takes another turn. If the player does not have a match, both cards are placed face down in the original position on the grid. Play until all uppercase letters have been paired with their lowercase matches. The player with the most matched pairs in the winner!

Letter-Attribute Sort: On the photocopier, enlarge the uppercase and lowercase numbered letters that appear at the top-left of each manuscript practice page onto heavy construction paper. Cut horizontally between the uppercase and lowercase letters, making each into a square-shaped card. Laminate. Have the students sort letters by appearance. For example, place all those letters with curves in one pile (e.g., uppercase and lowercase *Cc*, *Oo*, lowercase *g*), all those with straight lines in another pile (e.g., uppercase *A*, uppercase and lowercase *Tt*), and those with both curves and straight lines into a third pile (e.g., lowercase *a*, uppercase and lowercase *Bb*). When introducing this activity, you might consider dividing uppercase and lowercase letters into two separate categories. As students become more confident with the alphabet, you can mix the uppercase and lowercase categories together.

Name

A

1. From the top to the bottom
2. From the top to the bottom
3. Across the middle

a

1. Around in a circle
2. Up, then down

Aa

is for ant.

A A A A A

A

a a a a a a a

a

Name

B

1. From the top to the bottom
2. Around into the middle
3. Around to the bottom

b

1. From the top to the bottom
2. Up and around to the right

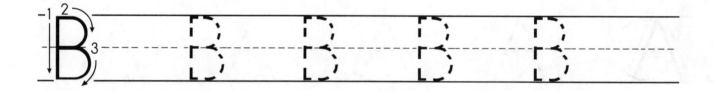

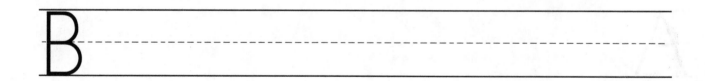

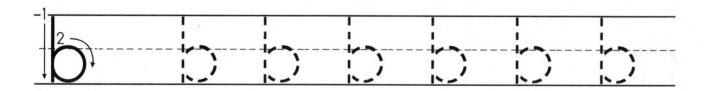

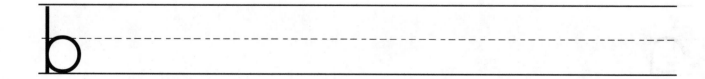

B B B B B

B

b b b b b b b

b

Name

C

1. Curve up to the top, then around to the bottom

c

1. Curve up to the middle, then around to the bottom

Cc

is for cat.

C

C

c

c

Name

D

1. From the top to the bottom
2. Back to the top, then around and down

d

1. Around in a circle to the left
2. Up to the top, then down to the bottom

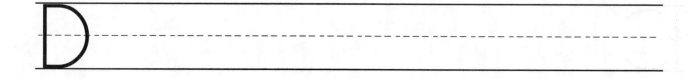

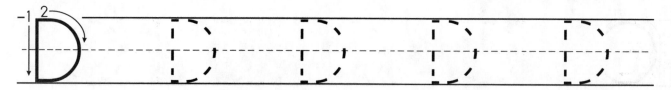

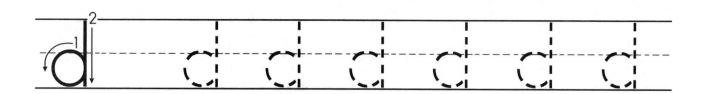

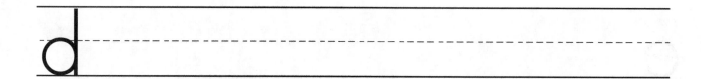

Dd

is for dog.

D D D D D

D

d d d d d d d

d

Name

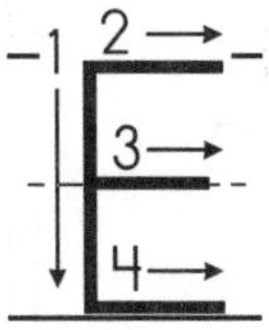

1. From the top to the bottom
2. Across the top
3. Across the middle
4. Across the bottom

1. A line across
2. Up and over to the middle then around to the bottom

Ee

is for egg.

E

e

Name

1. From the top to the bottom
2. Across the top
3. Across the middle

1. Curve around to the top, then down to the bottom
2. Across the middle

Ff

is for frog.

Name

1. Curve up to the top, then around to the bottom, then up
2. Across the middle

1. Around in a circle to the left
2. Up, then down below the line, and make a left hook

Gg

is for goose.

Name

H

1. From the top to the bottom
2. From the top to the bottom
3. Across the middle

h

1. From the top to the bottom
2. Up, over, and down

Hh

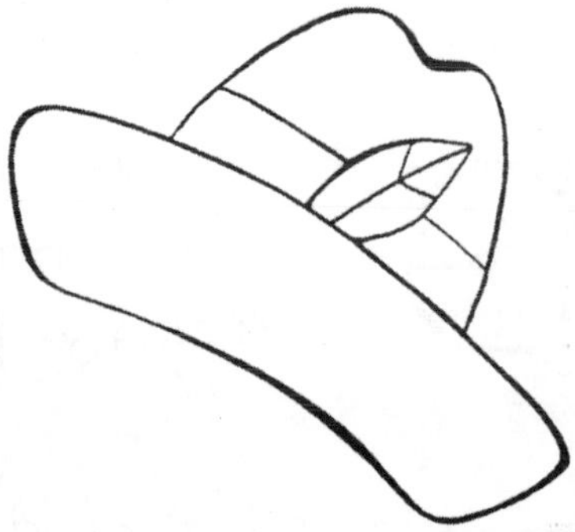

is for hat.

H H H H H

H

h h h h h h h

h

Name

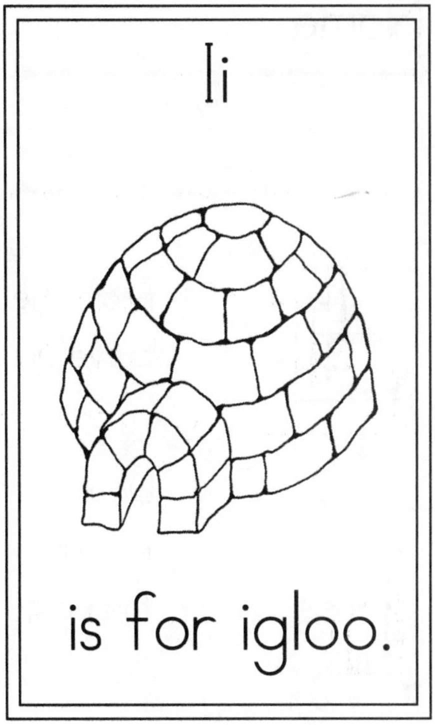

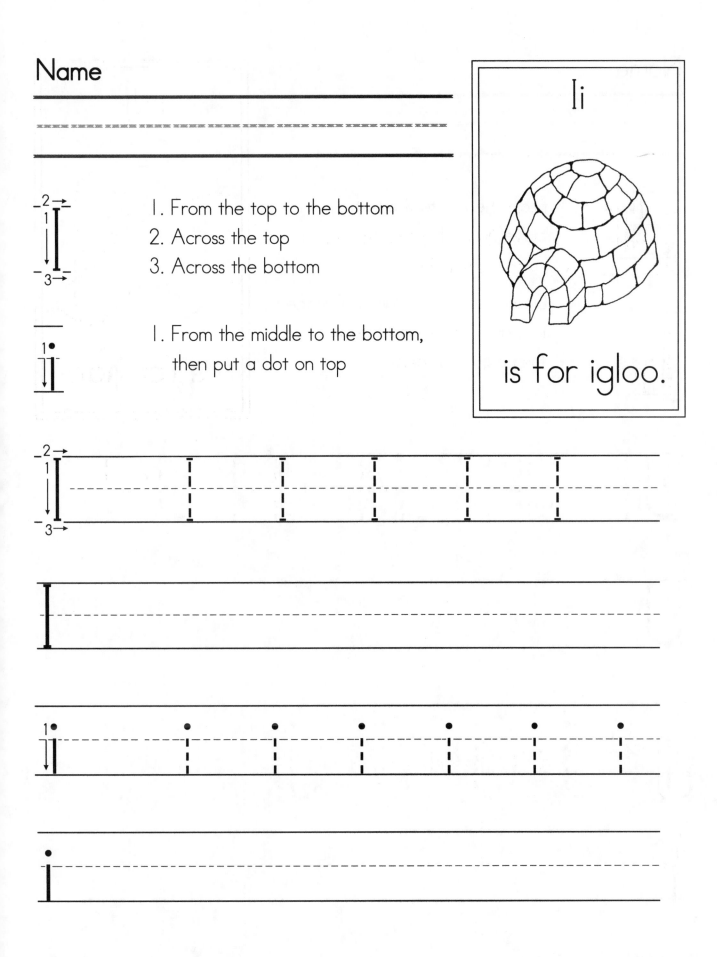

1. From the top to the bottom
2. Across the top
3. Across the bottom

1. From the middle to the bottom, then put a dot on top

Name

1. From the top to the bottom, then curve up to the left

1. Down from the middle, below the line, and make a hook to the left, then put a dot on top

Name

1. From the top to the bottom
2. From the top to the middle
3. From the middle to the bottom

1. From the top to the bottom
2. From the middle in
3. Down to the bottom

Kk

is for kite.

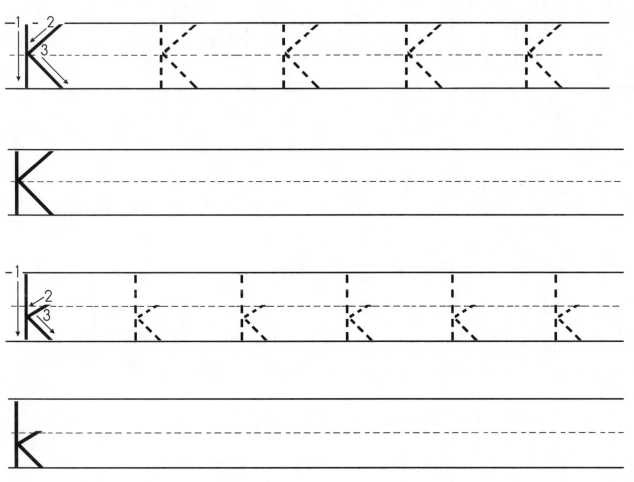

K

k

Name

1. From the top to the bottom
2. Across the bottom to the right

1. From the top to the bottom

Ll

is for lion.

Name

-1 3 — 4 2-

M

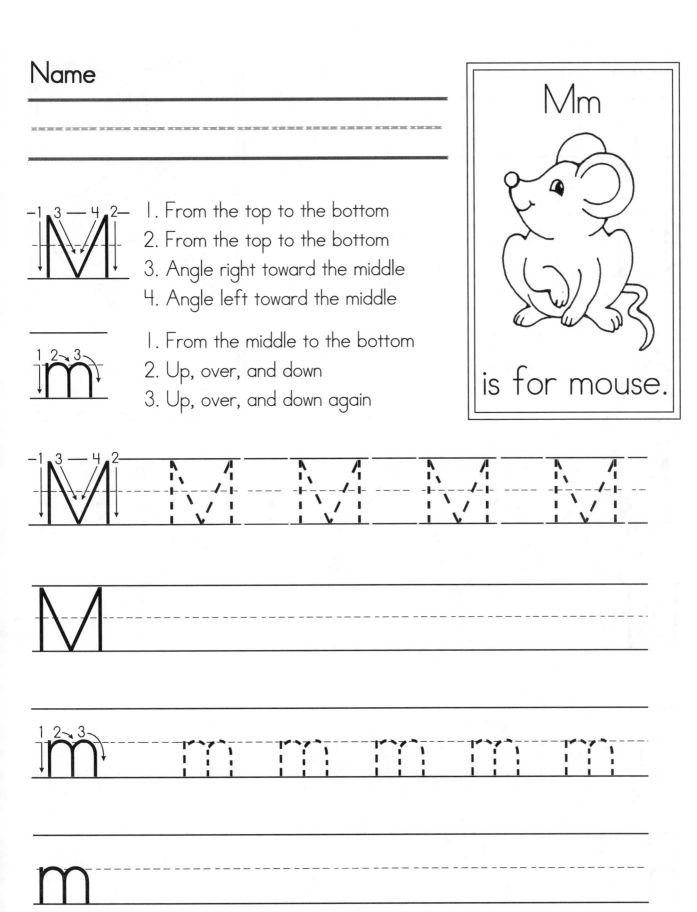

1. From the top to the bottom
2. From the top to the bottom
3. Angle right toward the middle
4. Angle left toward the middle

1 2 3

m

1. From the middle to the bottom
2. Up, over, and down
3. Up, over, and down again

Mm

is for mouse.

-1 3 — 4 2

M

M

1 2 3

m

m

Name

N

1. From the top to the bottom
2. From the top to the bottom
3. Slant top to bottom

n

1. From the middle to the bottom
2. Up, over, and down

Nn

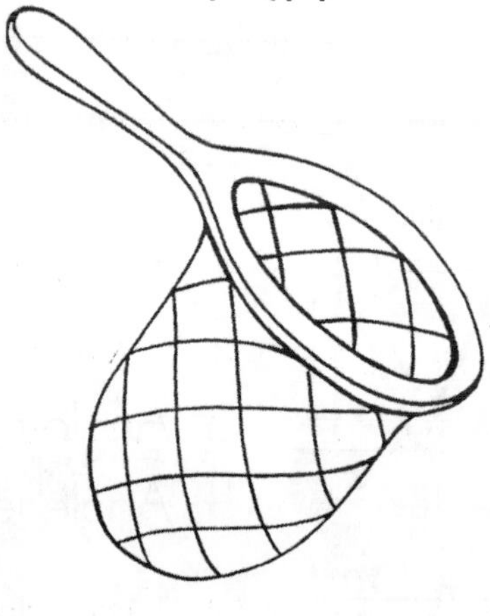

is for net.

N N N N N

N

n n n n n n n

n

Name

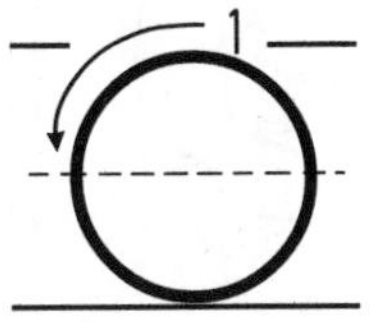

1. From the top
around to the bottom, then
around to the top

1. From the middle
around to the bottom, then
around to the middle

Name

Pp

is for pig.

P

1. From the top to the bottom
2. From the top around to the middle

p

1. From the middle straight down past the line
2. Up, then around to the right

P P P P P

P

p p p p p p p

p

Name

1. Around to the bottom, then around to the top
2. Add a small line

1. Around in a circle to the left
2. Up, then down below the line, and make a small line up

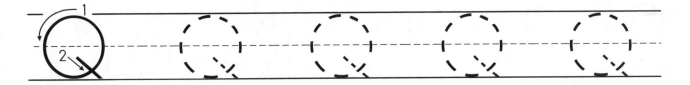

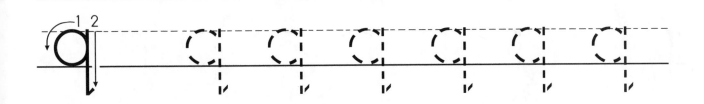

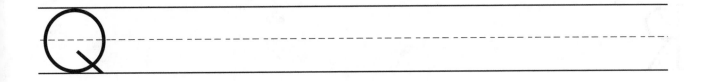

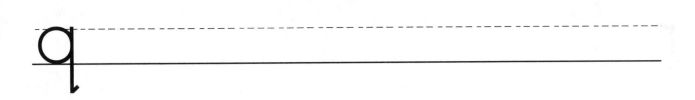

Qq

is for quail.

Name

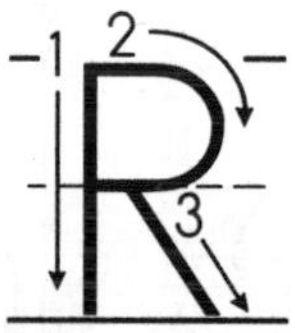

1. From the top to the bottom
2. From the top around to the middle
3. Down to the bottom

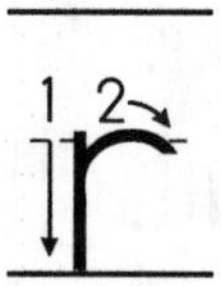

1. From the middle to the bottom
2. Up and curve to the right

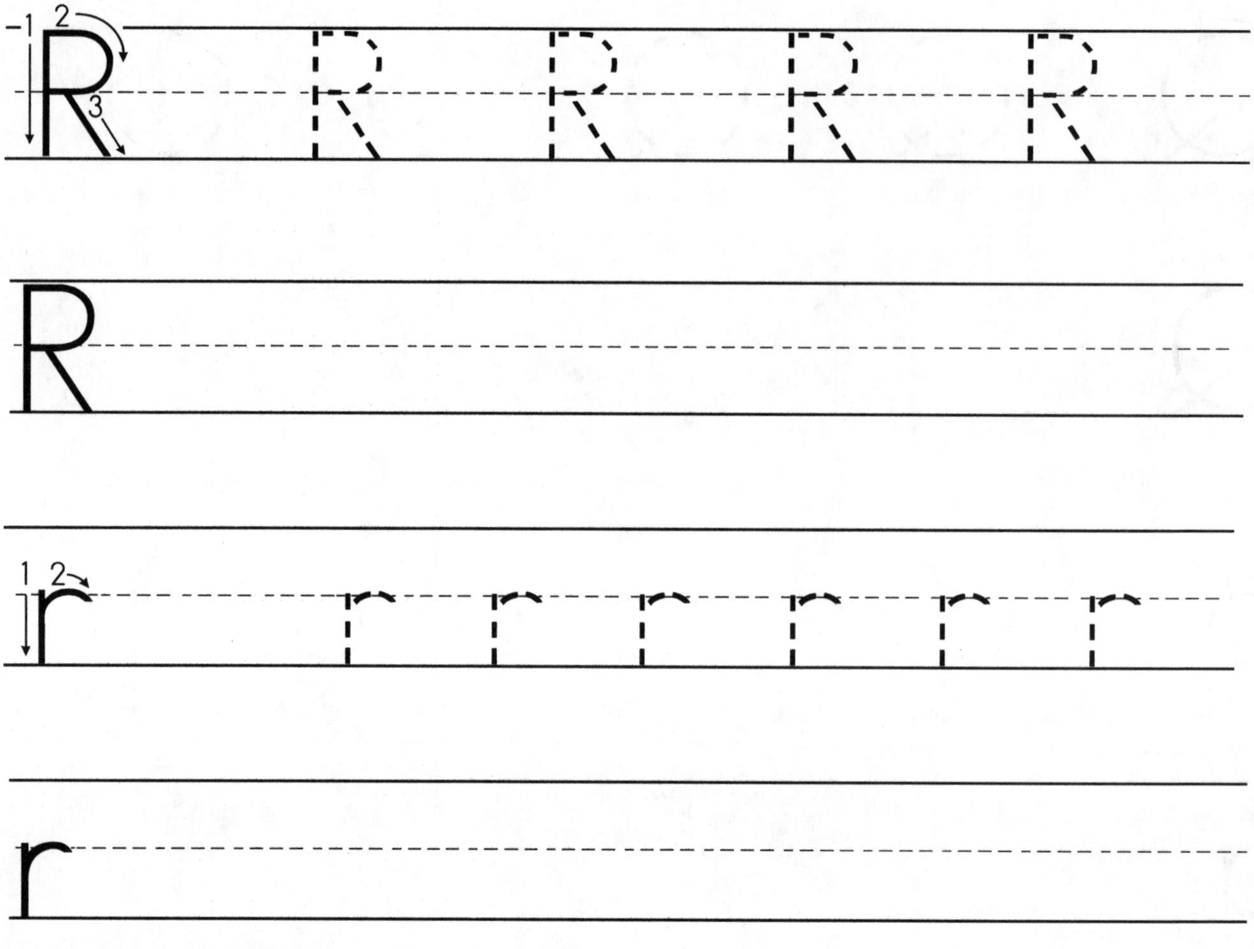

Name

S

1. Curve from the top to the middle, then change direction and curve down to the bottom and up

s

1. Curve down from the middle, then change direction and curve down to the bottom and up

Ss

is for sun.

S S S S S

S

s s s s s s s s

s

Name

1. From the top to the bottom
2. Across the top

1. Down to the bottom
2. Across the middle

Tt

is for tree.

Name

U

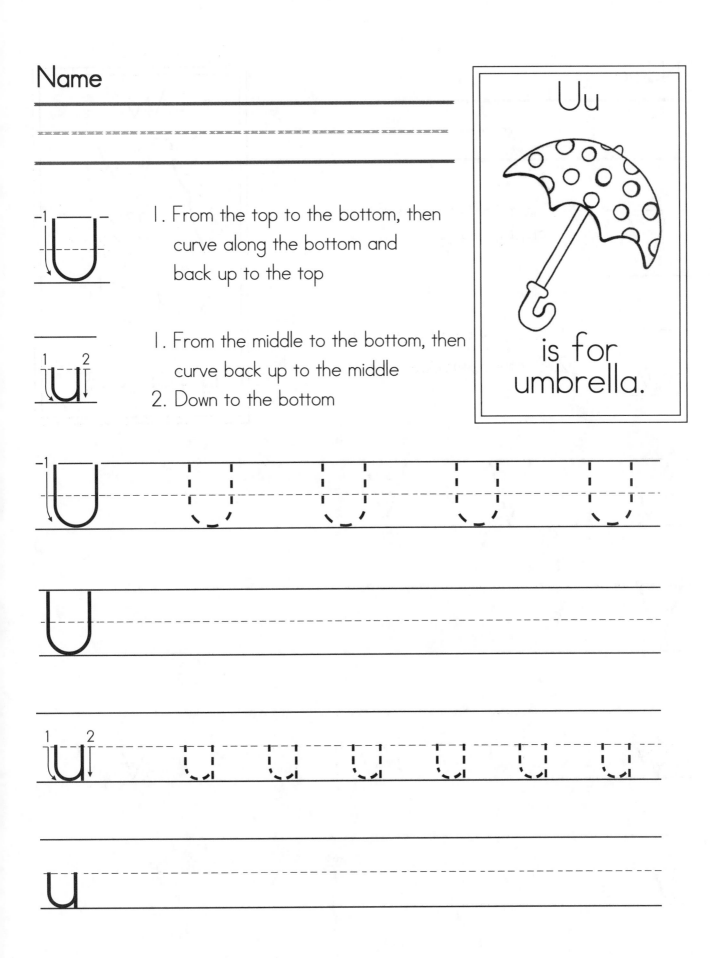

1. From the top to the bottom, then curve along the bottom and back up to the top

u

1. From the middle to the bottom, then curve back up to the middle
2. Down to the bottom

Uu

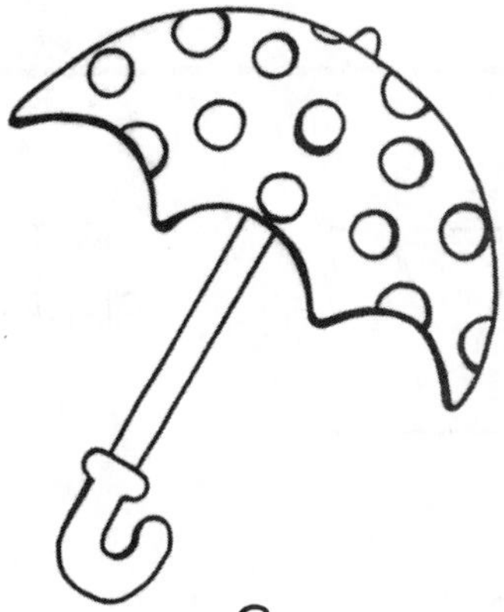

is for umbrella.

U

U

u

u

Name

Vv

is for vest.

V

1. Slant right, top to bottom
2. Slant left, top to bottom

v

1. Slant right, middle to bottom
2. Slant left, middle to bottom

V V V V V

V

v v v v v v v

v

Name

-1 —2 3— 4-

W

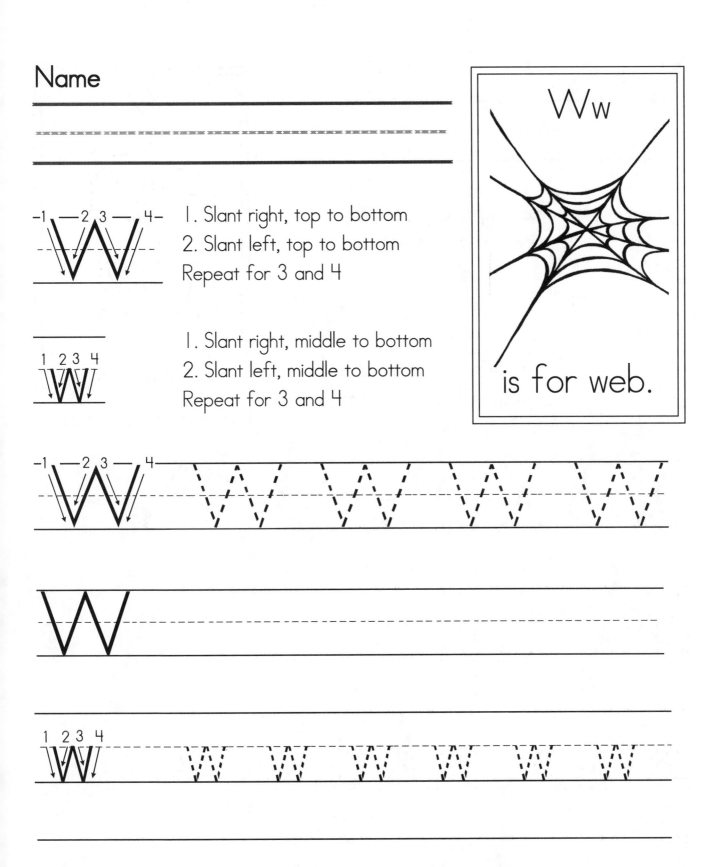

1. Slant right, top to bottom
2. Slant left, top to bottom
Repeat for 3 and 4

1 2 3 4

w

1. Slant right, middle to bottom
2. Slant left, middle to bottom
Repeat for 3 and 4

Ww

is for web.

-1 —2 3— 4-

W W W W W

W

1 2 3 4

w w w w w w w

w

Name

X

1. Slant right, top to bottom
2. Slant left, top to bottom
(The lines should cross in the middle.)

x

1. Slant right, middle to bottom
2. Slant left, middle to bottom
(The lines should cross in the middle.)

Xx

is for box.

X X X X X

X

x x x x x x x x

x

Name

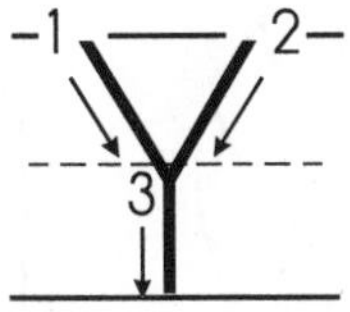

1. Slant right, top to middle
2. Slant left, top to middle
3. Straight down to the bottom

1. Slant right, middle to bottom
2. Slant left from the middle, then down below the line

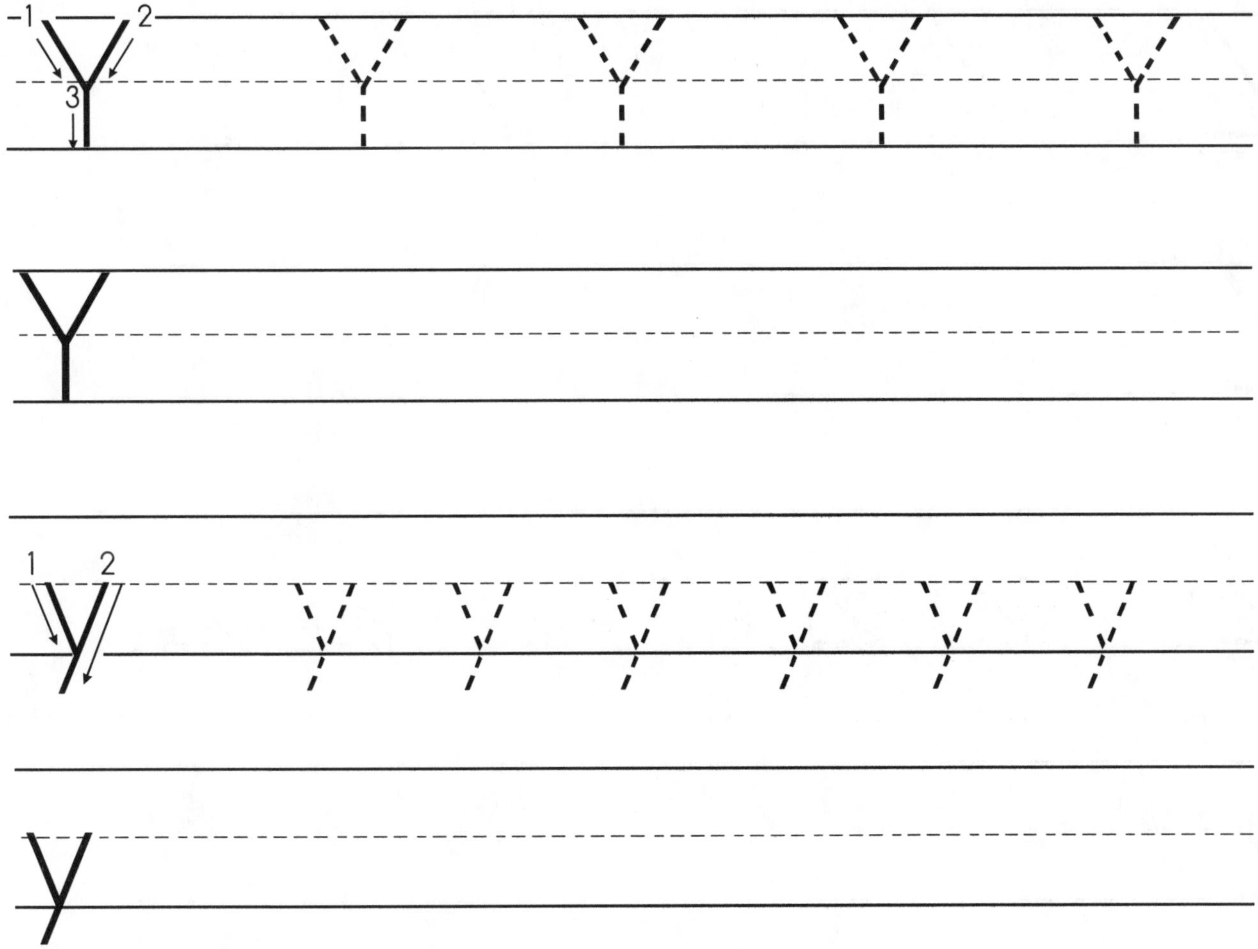

Name

1. Across the top, then
slant left top to bottom, then
across the bottom

1. Across the middle, then
slant left middle to bottom, then
across the bottom

Zz

is for zebra.

ABC Alphacards: Multipurpose Alphabet Cards with Picture Cues

There are many fun and exciting ways to incorporate "ABC Alphacards" into your literacy program. These cards are extremely beneficial for students at the emergent level who are beginning to establish letter/sound relationships. Following you will find a variety of applications and directions for the use of these cards.

HATS: Photocopy the Alphacard patterns on white or colored construction paper. Have students color and cut them out. Staple onto a 2" x 18" strip of construction paper to fit.

FLASH CARDS: Photocopy the Alphacard patterns on card stock or construction paper, then cut and color, if desired. You may give each student cards to practice with at home, or you can laminate them for in-class use at an alphabet center or as part of a tutoring activity.

INDIVIDUAL ALPHABET BOOKS: Photocopy the Alphacard patterns, cut the pages in half so that one letter is on each half sheet of paper, then have each child color a complete set, A to Z. Now, bind the pages into book form using staples or a comb binding.

STICK PUPPETS: Glue or staple a craft stick onto the back of each Alphacard after students have colored them and you have cut them out. Use these Alphacard puppets to introduce or emphasize each new letter.

ALPHABET LINE: Copy, color, cut, and display Alphacards, in alphabetical order, on a classroom wall or bulletin board. Post the alphabet line in its entirety before school begins, or build it as you introduce each new letter.

WORD WALL: Post each Alphacard on a bulletin board, wall, or long sheet of butcher paper. Then place high-frequency words, student names, or vocabulary words on sentence strips, file cards, or light-colored construction paper as you introduce them to the class. Place each word under the Alphacard letter that begins the word. For example, the words *Allison, and, a* and *an* would be placed under the *Aa* Alphacard.

COLORING BOOK: Copy and bind Alphacards into book form for children to color either at an alphabet center or individually.

Aa

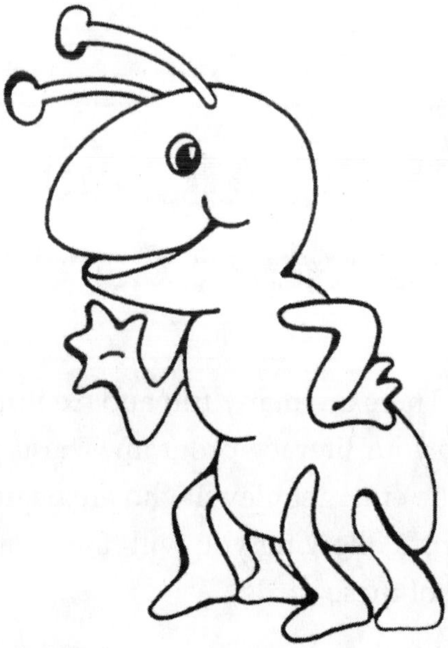

Bb

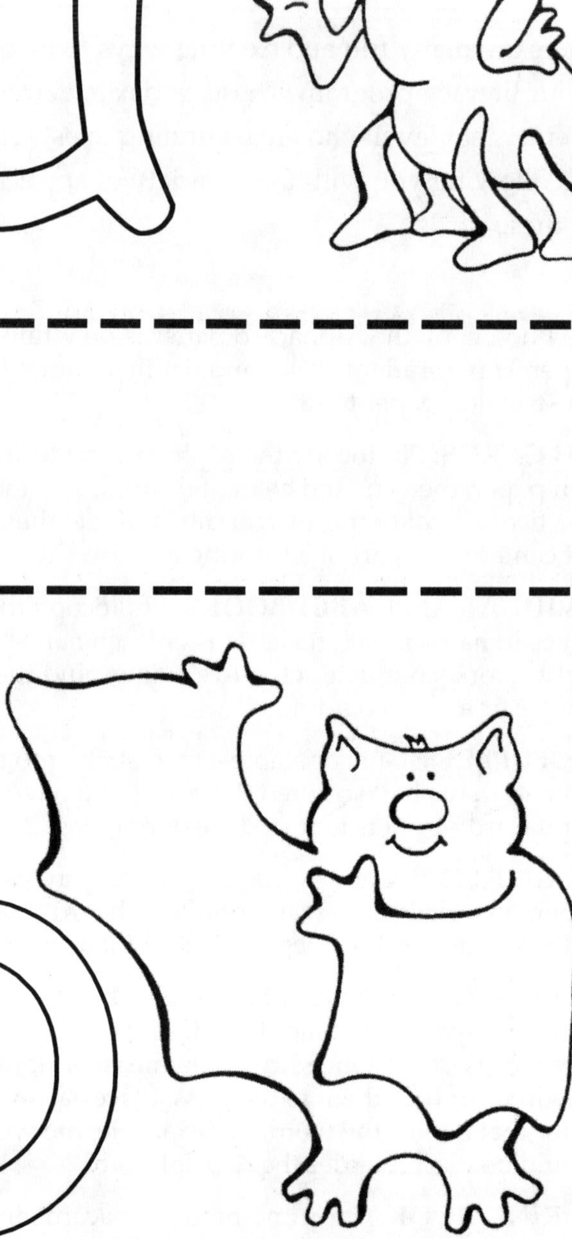

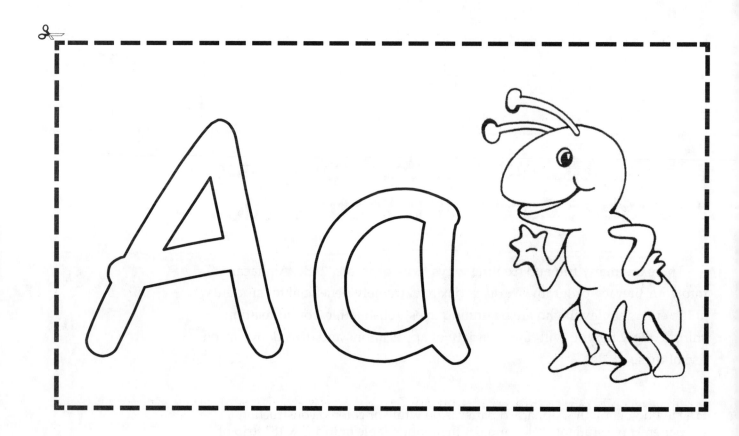

Cc

Dd

Ee

Ff

Gg

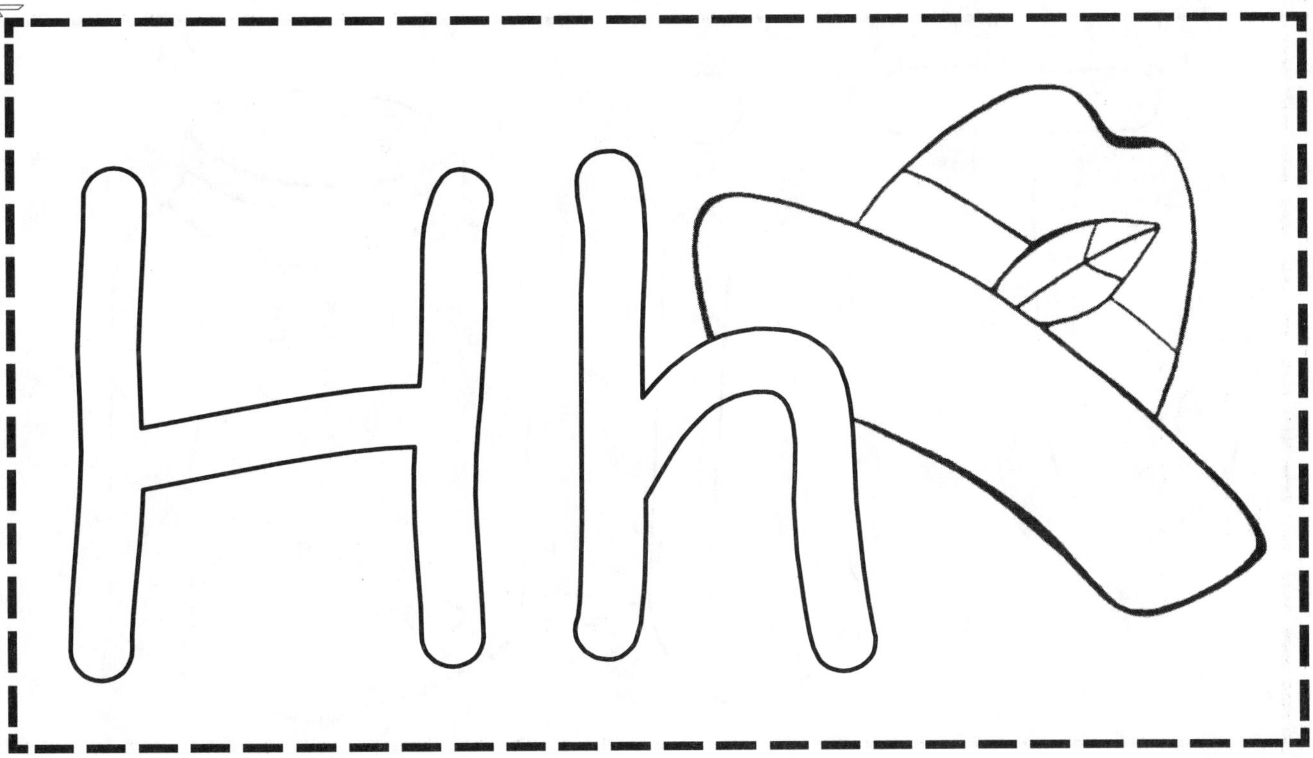
Hh

I i

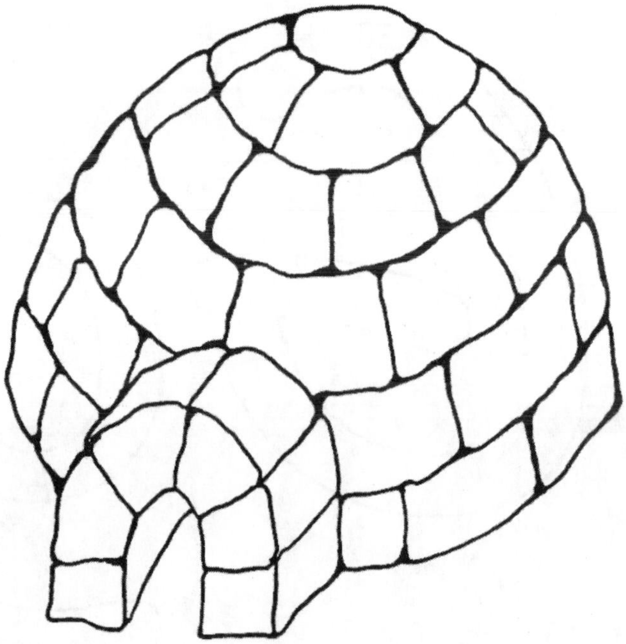

J j

Kk

Ll

Mm

Nn

Oo

Pp

Qq

Rr

Ss 

Tt 

Uu

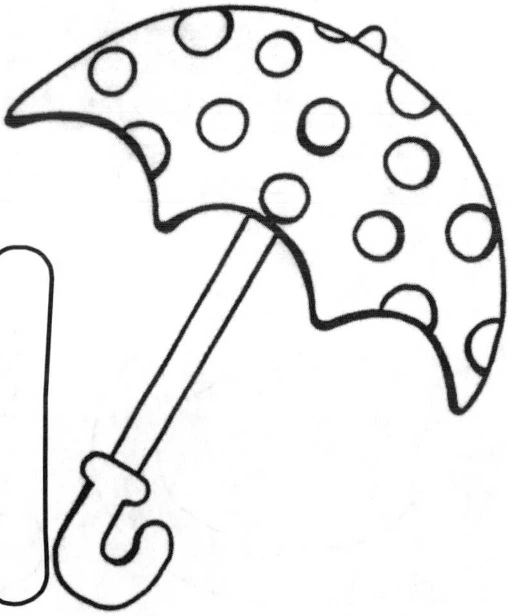

Vv

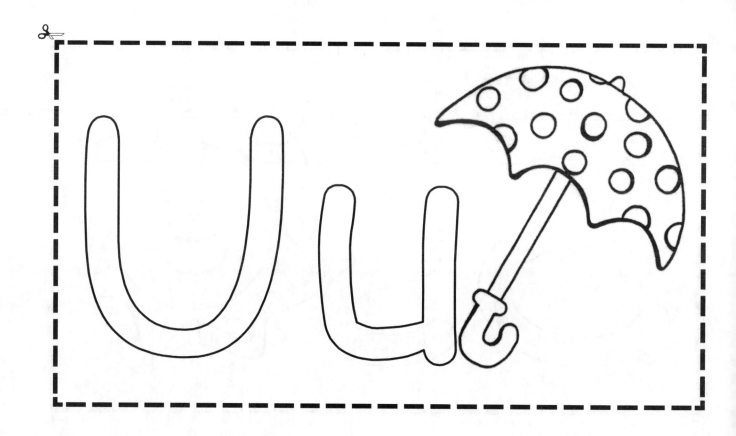

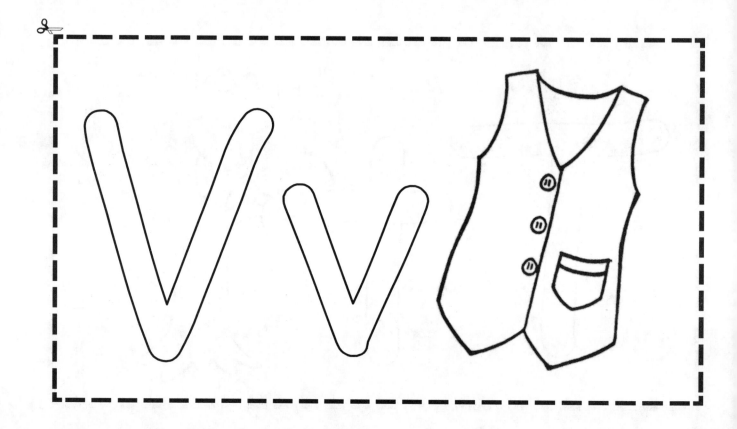

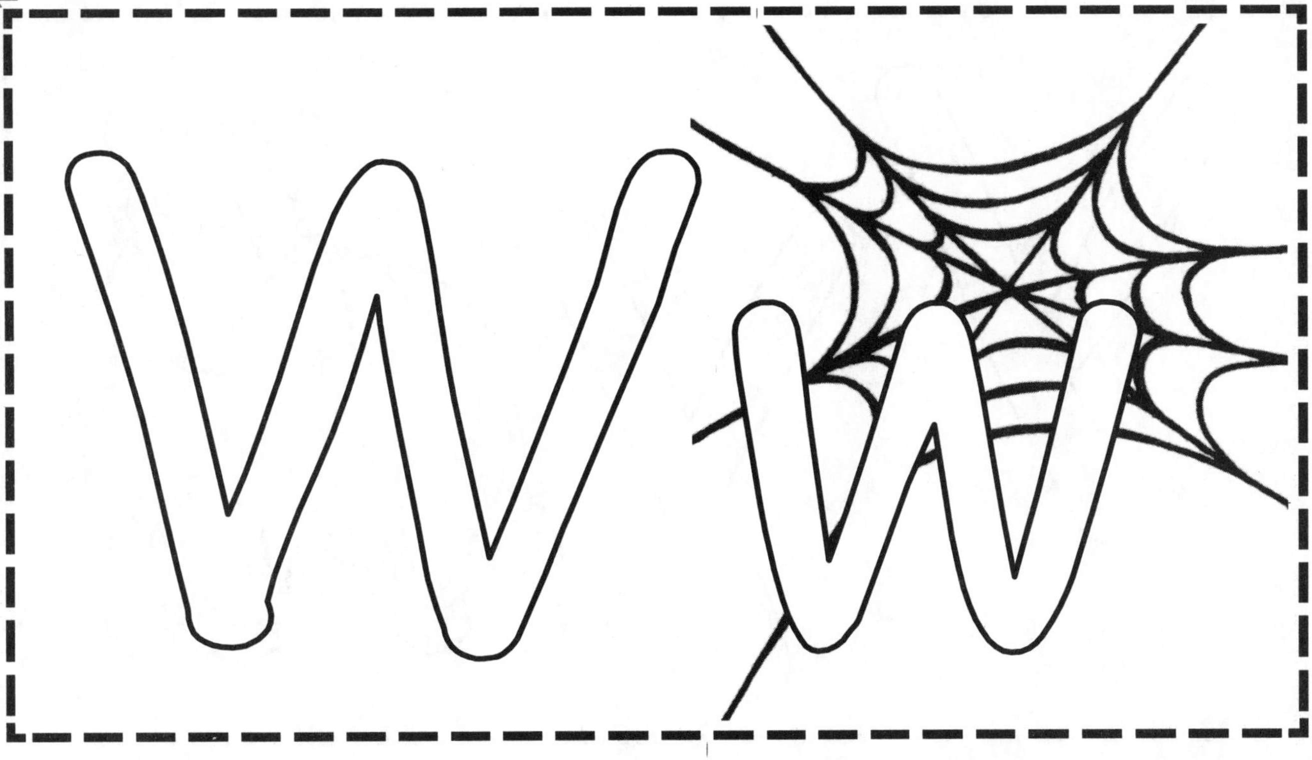
Ww

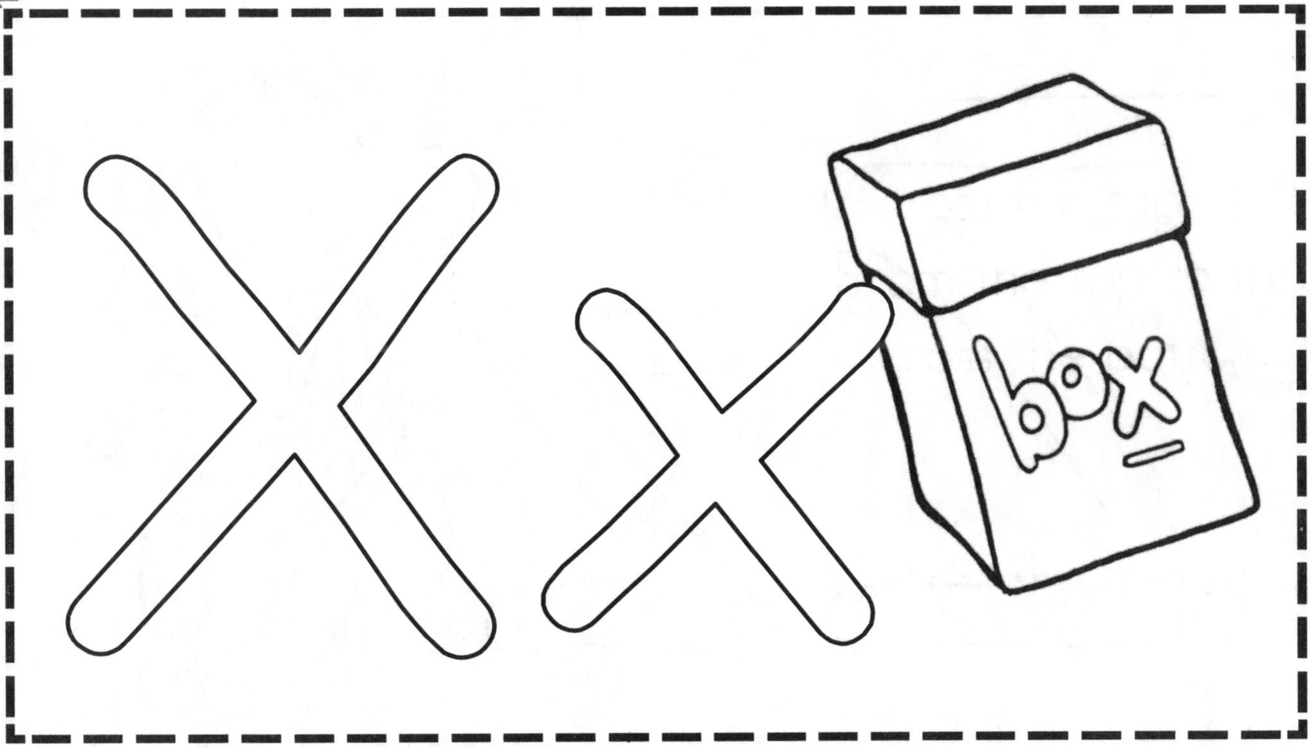
Xx
box

Yy

Zz

Section 4

ABC Read with Me: Early Emergent Level Books Focusing on Letter/Sound Recognition

These early emergent level alphabet books are intended to be a supplemental activity to classroom instruction and curriculum, and are designed to strengthen students' skills in the following areas: letter/ sound recognition, print concept, and book-handling.

"ABC Read with Me" books are easy to make and store. Simply photocopy each page and quarter-fold it, as if you were making a greeting card. Have each student color and read the book to you. Be sure to check that each student is touch-tapping the words as s/he reads. These books may be stored in Ziploc bags or individual student tubs or cubbies for frequent reading access. Students are sure to find joy and reading confidence in the library of books they create.

Activities for Early Emergent Level Books

The following activities are great for either individual or small-group use and are perfect for your literacy centers. There are many different activities you and your students can create, so brainstorm together and have fun!

Photocopy and laminate each unfolded early emergent book page as follows:

1. On the cover page (e.g., *Aa, Bb, Cc*) cover the word *"by"* and the line meant for student names with Wite-Out, white Post-it Tape, or a piece of paper, cut to match, securely affixed before you photocopy each page.

2. With scissors or a paper cutter, cut down the center of the page then across the middle. You should have four separate cards for each letter (illustrations with corresponding sentences and one letter card).

3. Laminate and trim these cards.

4. Separate the letter cards from picture/sentence cards. Keep the letter cards in alphabetical order and store in Ziploc bags.

Matching/Sequence Game

- Shuffle the picture/sentence cards well.
- Place a letter card at the top of a pocket chart and have students sift through the pile of picture/sentence cards until they find the three cards that correspond with the featured letter card in the pocket chart. If working with a student one-on-one, you may simply place the letter card on the table while you and the student sift through the cards together.
- Continue on in this manner, using all the letter cards and matching picture/sentence cards.

Match and Label

- Follow the photocopying instructions above, but this time also cover the sentences with Wite-Out, white Post-it Tape, or paper before you photocopy.
- Place a letter card at the top of the pocket chart.
- Sift through the picture cards until you find one that starts with the corresponding letter (e.g., *Apple* for *Aa*). Ask students what sounds they hear in the word and using a water-soluble pen, label the picture.
- Place the labeled picture card below the letter card.
- Continue on in this manner until students have found the two remaining cards.

This is an astronaut.

This is an alligator.

Aa

This is an apple.

by: ____________________

Here is a bed.

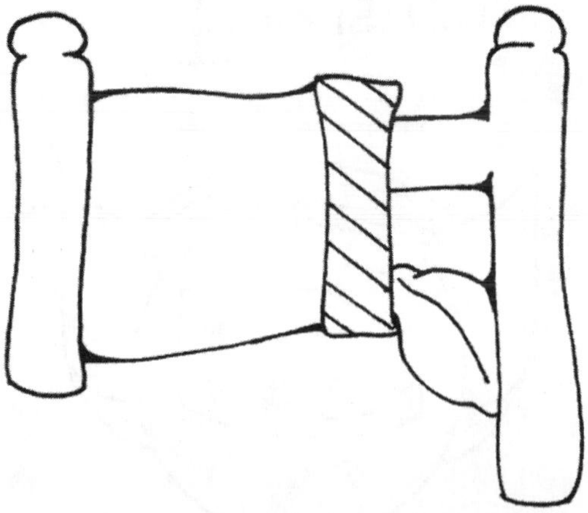

Here is a bird.

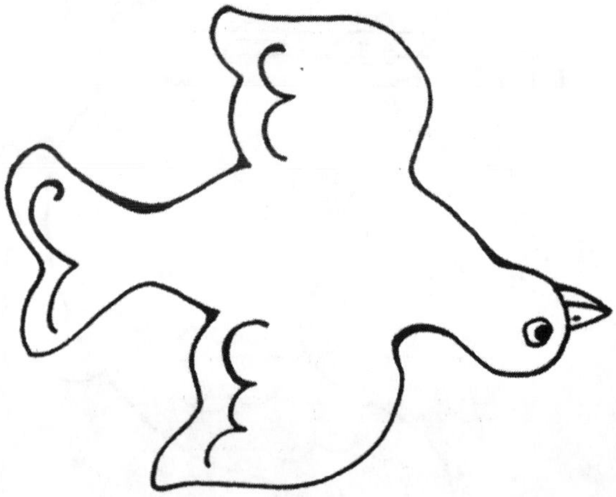

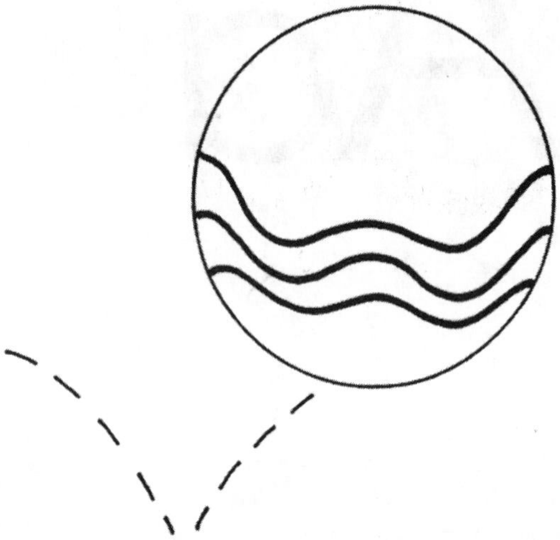

Bb

Here is a ball.

by: ______________

Look at the cup.

Look at the car.

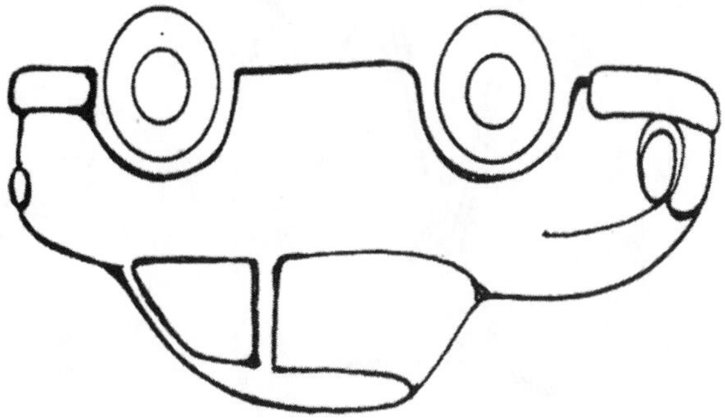

Cc

Look at the cat. by: ____________________

See the drum.

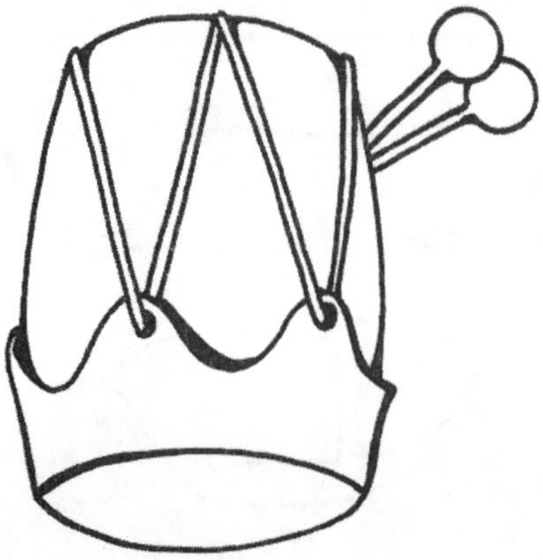

See the doll.

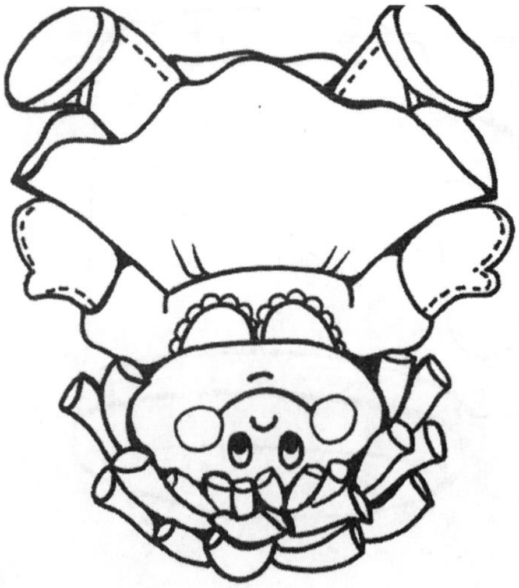

Dd

by: ____________________

See the dog.

Ee

by: ____________________

This is an egg.

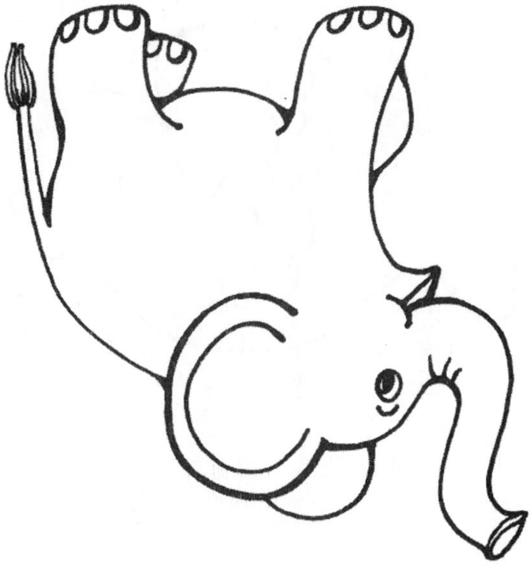

This is an elephant.

This is an elbow.

Look, a fish.

Look, a flag.

Ff

Look, a feather.

by: ____________________

Here is a girl.

Here is a garden.

Here is a goat.

Gg

by: ____________________

See the horse.

See the hand.

Hh

by: ____________________

See the house.

This is an iguana.

This is an inchworm.

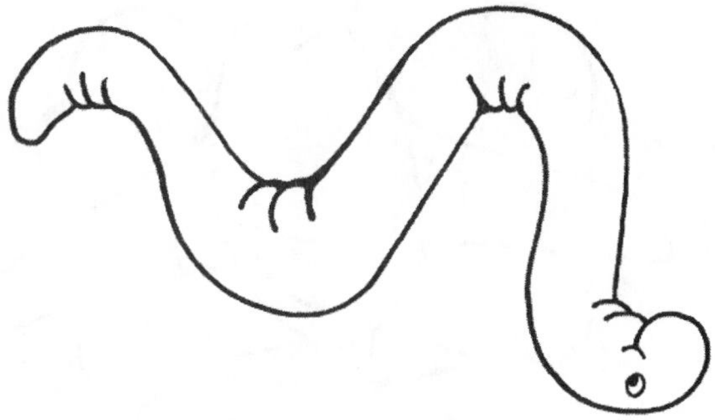

Ii

by: ______________________

This is an igloo.

Look at the juggler.

Look at the jet.

Look at the jar.

Jj

by: ____________________

Here is a key.

Here is a kitten.

Here is a kite.

Kk

by: ______________________

This is a lion.

This is a lamp.

Ll

This is a leaf.

by: ____________________

See the mop.

See the mitt.

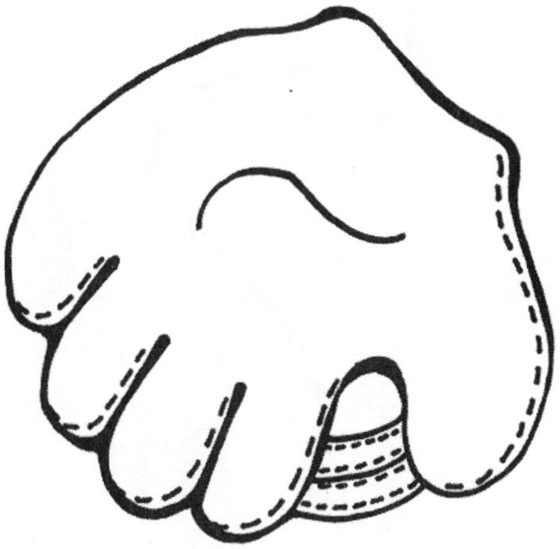

Mm

See the monkey. by: ____________________

Look, a nose.

Look, a nut.

Nn

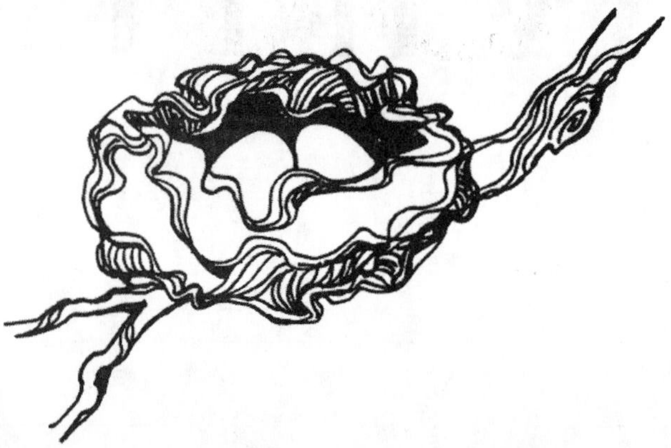

Look, a nest.

by: ____________________

Here is an olive.

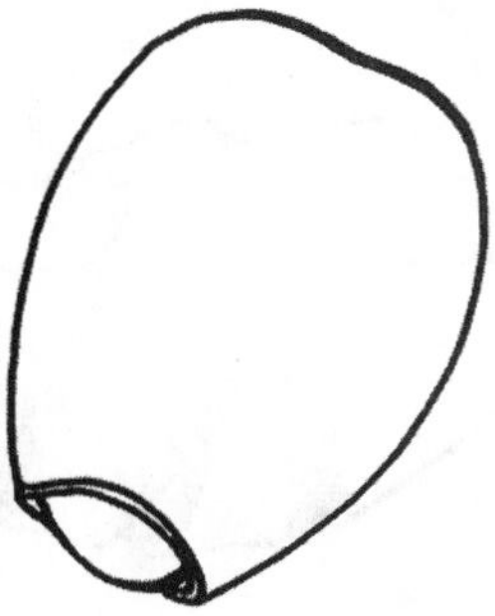

Here is an octopus.

Oo

Here is an ostrich.

by: ____________________

This is a pie.

This is a pear.

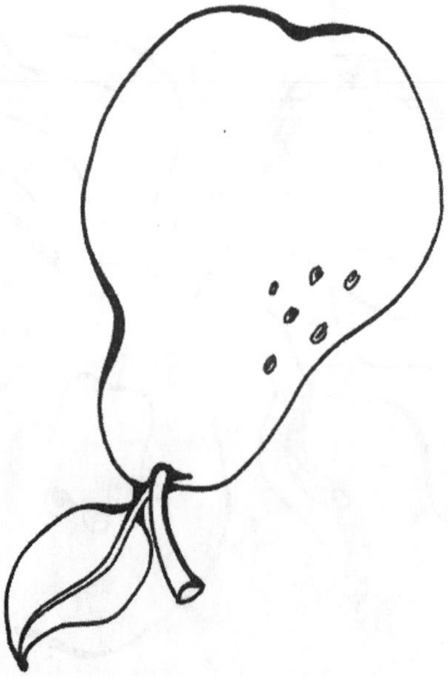

Pp

This is a pig.

by: ____________________

See the question mark.

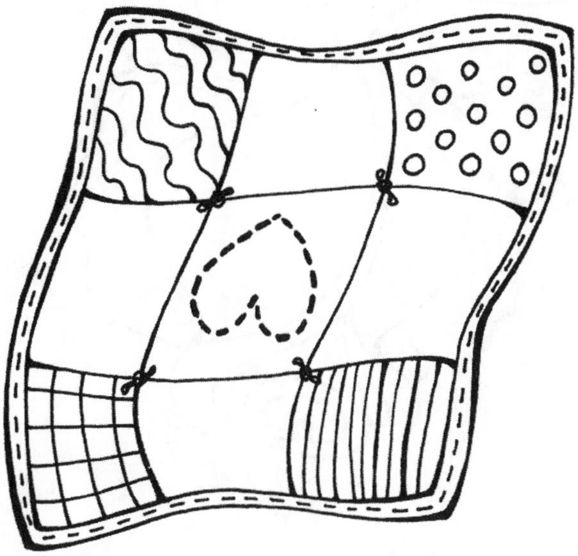

See the quilt.

Qq

by: ____________________

See the queen.

Rr

by: ____________________

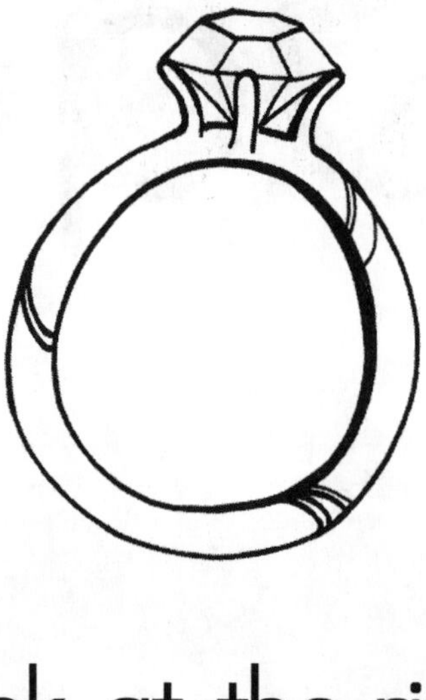

Look at the ring.

Look at the rabbit.

Look at the rose.

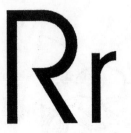

Here is the sun.

Here is a seal.

Here is a star.

Ss

by: ____________________

This is a turtle.

This is a tooth.

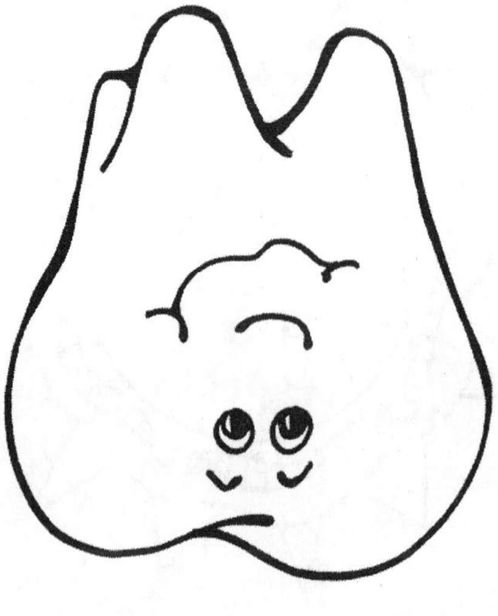

Tt

by: ____________________

This is a tiger.

Here is an uncle.

Here is an umpire.

Here is an umbrella.

Uu

by: ____________________

See the vest.

See the violin.

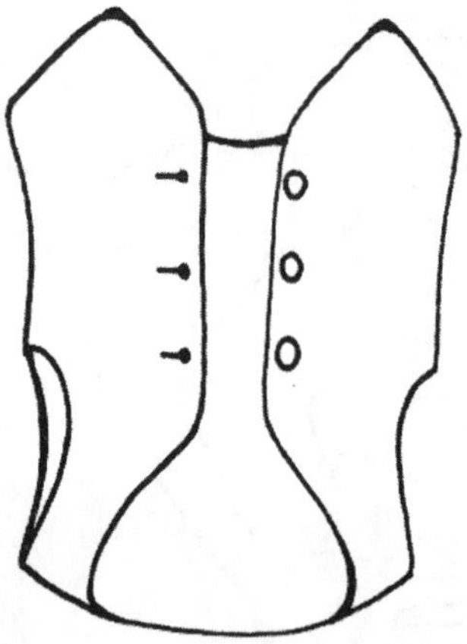

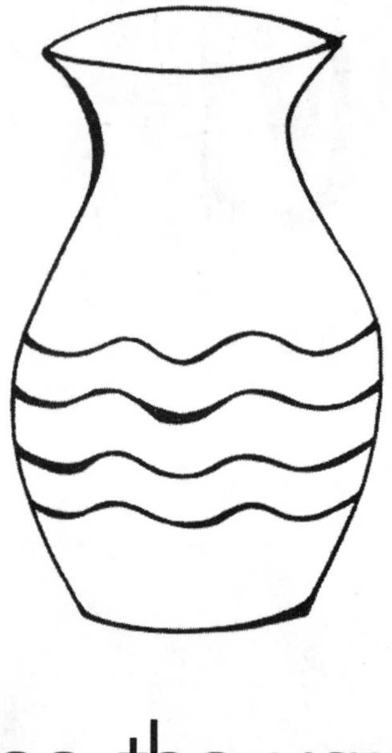

Vv

See the vase.

by: ____________________

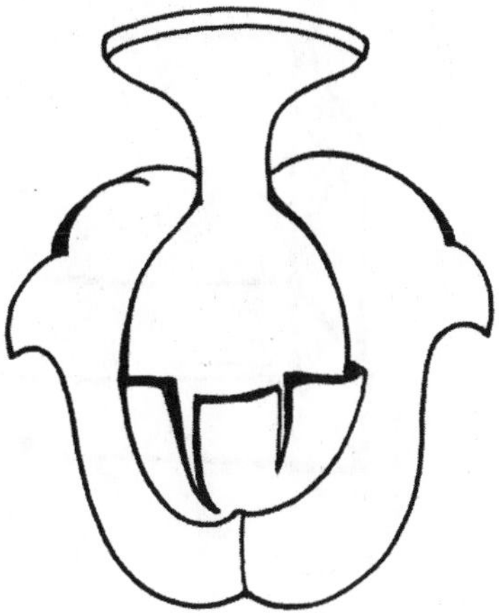

Look, a wig.

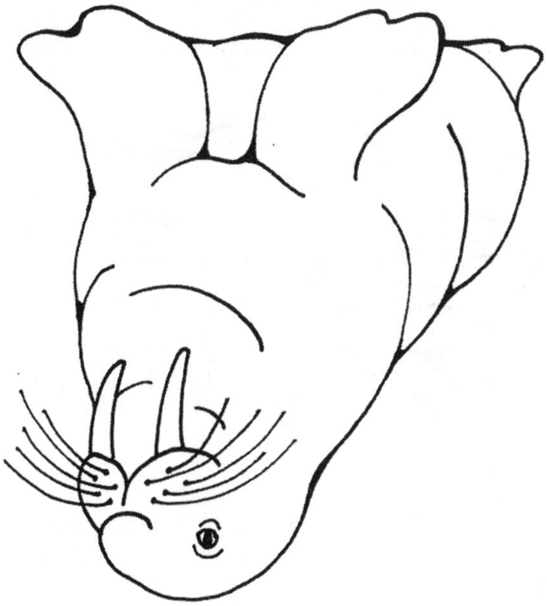

Look, a walrus.

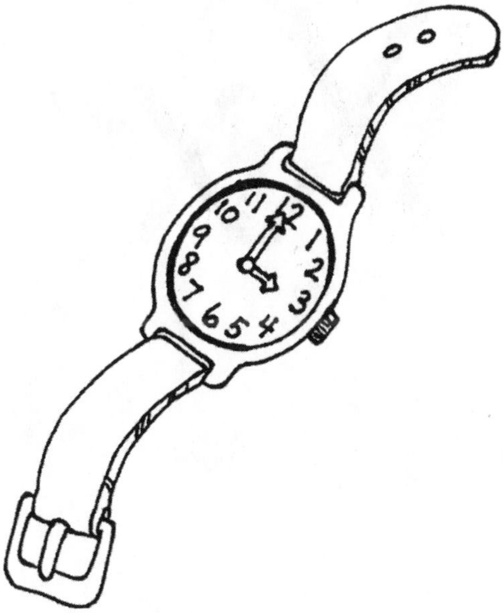

Ww

Look, a watch.

by: ____________________

See the ox.

See the box.

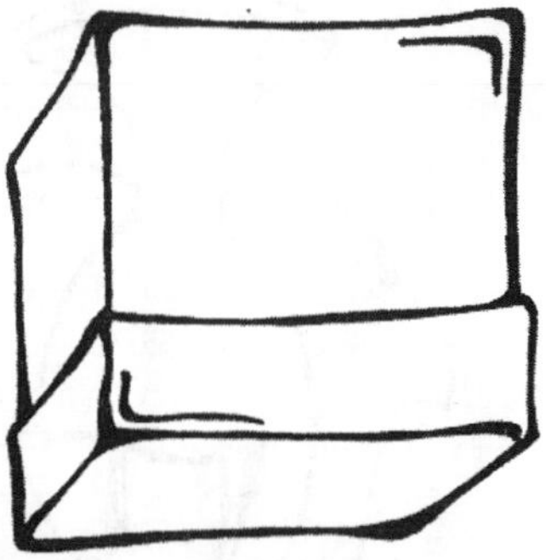

Xx

See the fox.

by: ____________________

This is a yell.

This is a yak.

Yy

This is a yo–yo.

by: ____________________

Here is a zoo.

Here is a zipper.

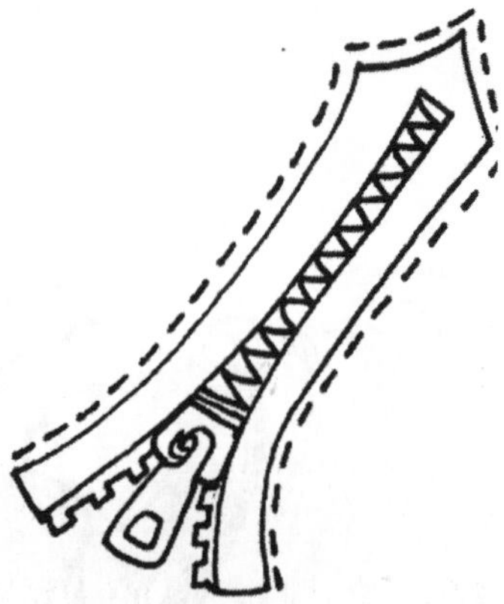

Here is a zebra.

Zz

by: ____________________

ABC Read with Me: Emergent Level Books Focusing on the Use of High-Frequency Words

The following emergent level alphabet books are intended to be a supplemental activity to classroom instruction and curriculum, and are designed to strengthen students' skills in the following areas: letter/sound recognition, print concepts, book-handling skills, and the knowledge and use of high-frequency words.

"ABC Read with Me" books are easy to create and store. Simply photocopy each page and quarter-fold it, as if you were making a greeting card. Have each student color and read the book to you. Be sure to check that each student is touch-tapping the words as s/he reads. These books may be stored in Ziploc bags or individual student tubs for easy access and frequent usage. Students are sure to find joy and reading confidence in the library of books they create.

Following are the emergent level alphabet book titles and the high-frequency words that may be found in each.

Ants

here

are

the

Bats

big

little

Cats

see

their

A Dog

a

can

Eggs

with

but

Frogs

them

just

The Goose
is
going
she

My Hats
this
is

My Igloo
it
made
to

Jars
of
on

The Kite
where
up

The Lion
I
have
what
am

The Mouse
he
came
for
then

In My Net
in
my
out
they
go

Octopus
that
make

Pigs
are

Quail
one
on

The Rabbit
his
very

The Sun
what
if

Trees
there

Umbrella
put
my
and

Vests
her
his
your

On a Web
who
make
has
look

Boxes
can't
play
but

Yaks
two
too

At the Zoo
you
will

Here are the red ants.

Here are the brown ants.

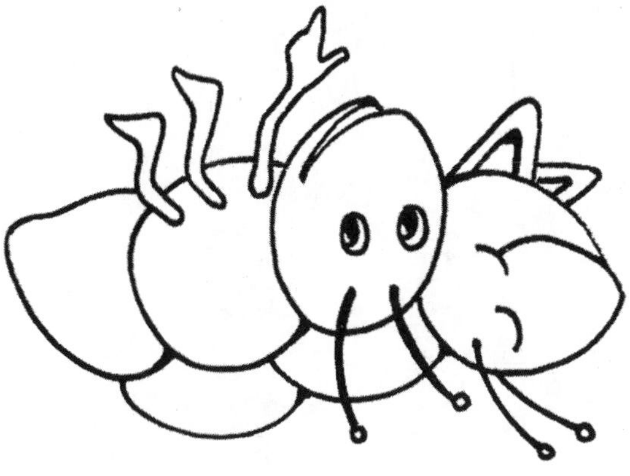

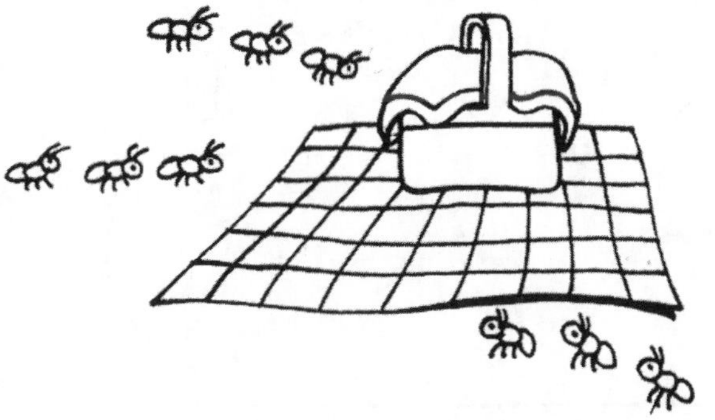

They are at our picnic.

Ants

____

Here are the black ants.

Bats

Big bat, little bat,

brown bat, black bat,

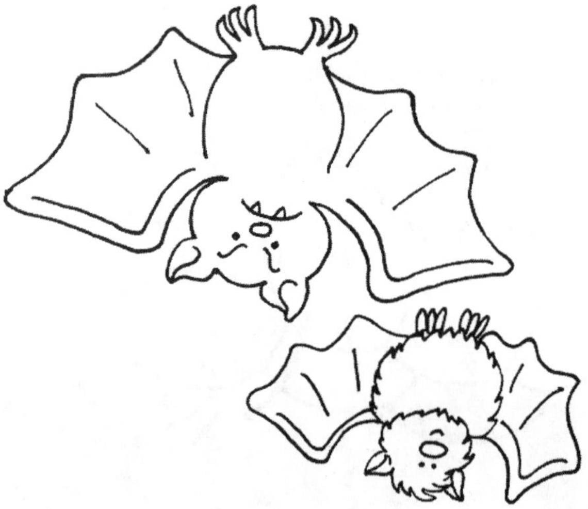

hairy bat, scary bat—

"Scat, bats! Scat!"

See the orange cat.

See the white cat.

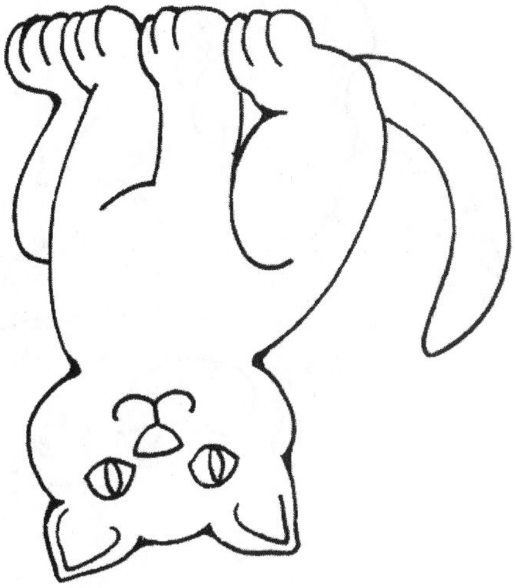

See their kittens.

Cats

See the black cat.

A dog can bark.

A dog can jump.

A Dog

"Down, boy! Down!"

A dog can sit.

Eggs

I like eggs with bacon.

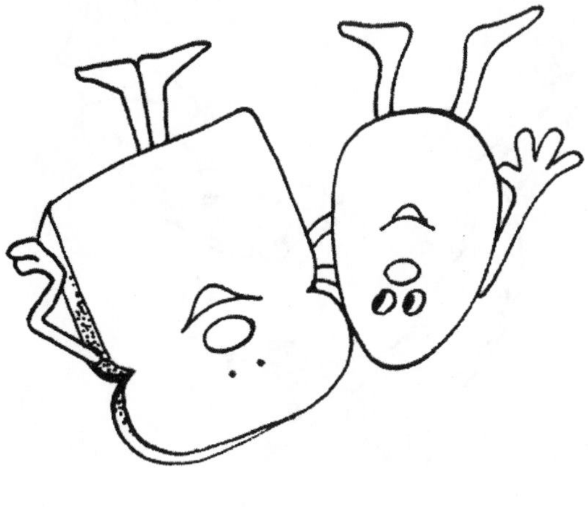

I like eggs with toast.

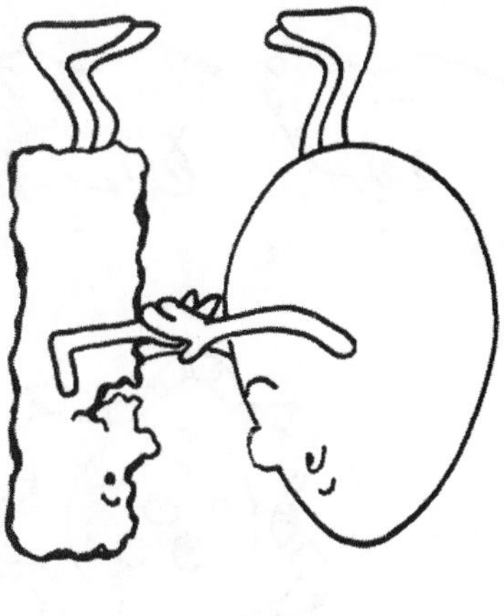

But eggs with sausage

I like most.

Frogs

See them sit.

See them swim.

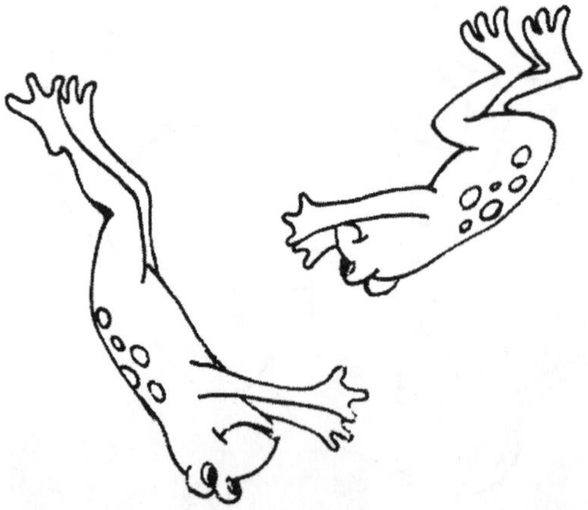

See them hop—

just in time!

The goose is going everywhere.

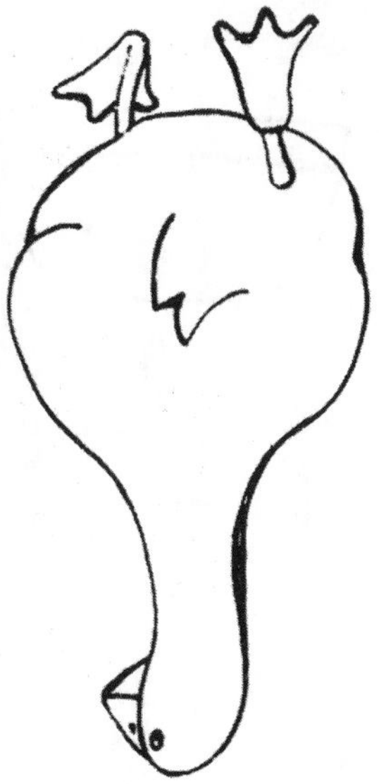

The goose is going there.

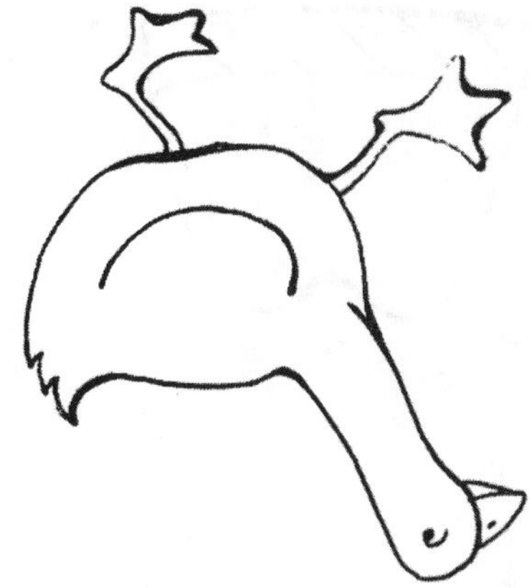

The Goose

She is chasing after me.

The goose is going here.

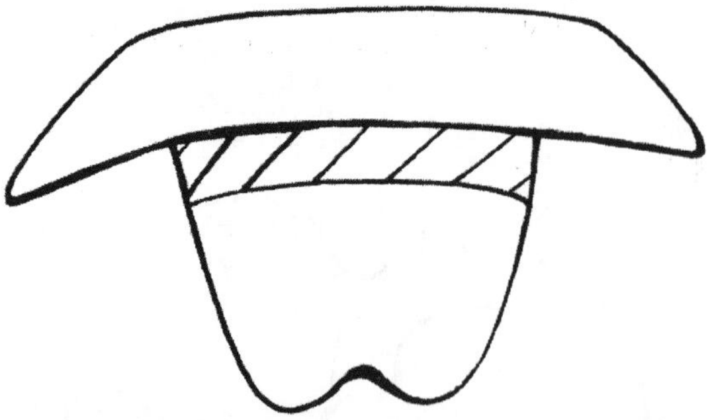

This is a wide hat.

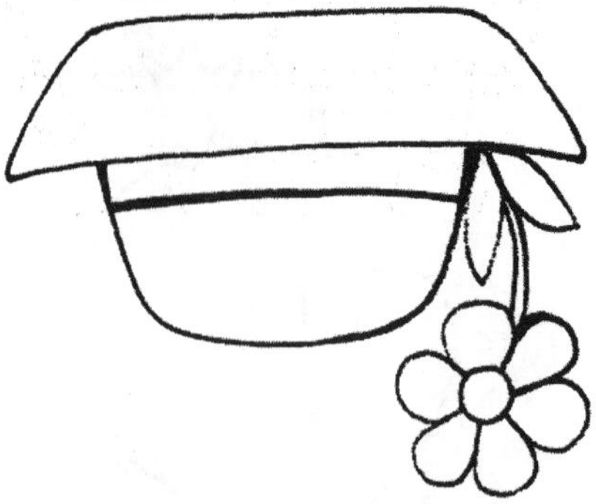

This is a short hat.

I like my hats.

My Hats

This is a tall hat.

It is made of blocks.

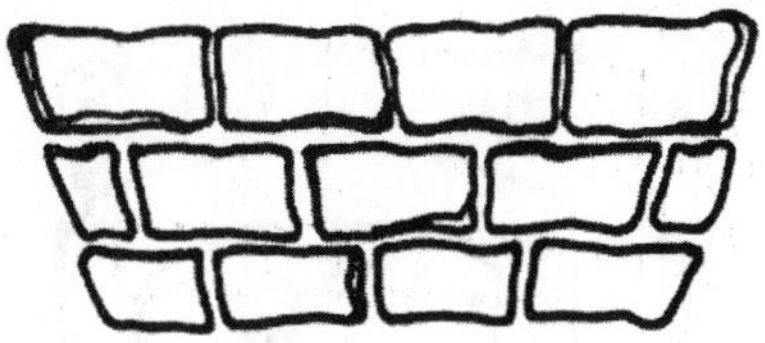

It is made of snow.

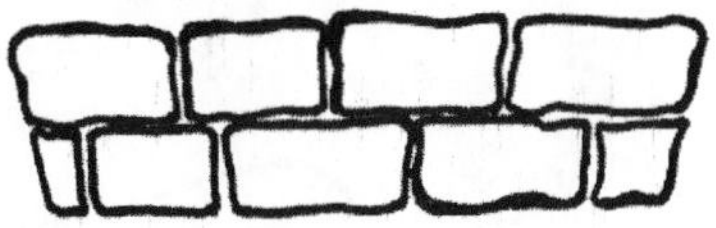

Welcome to my igloo.

My Igloo

It is made of ice.

I spread it on bread.

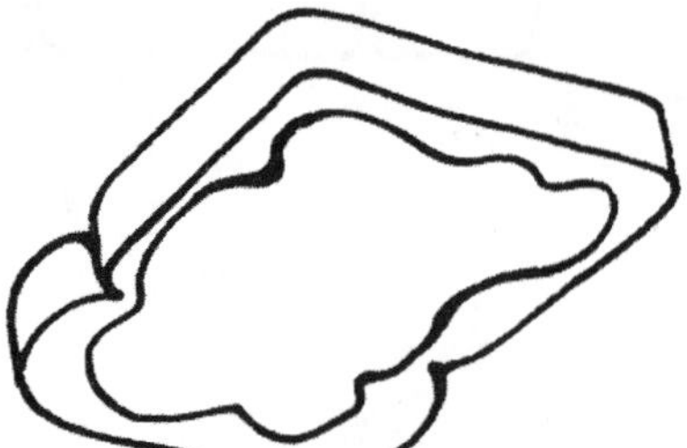

This is a jar of jelly.

Now it's in my belly!

Jars

____

This is a jar of peanut butter.

Where is the kite?

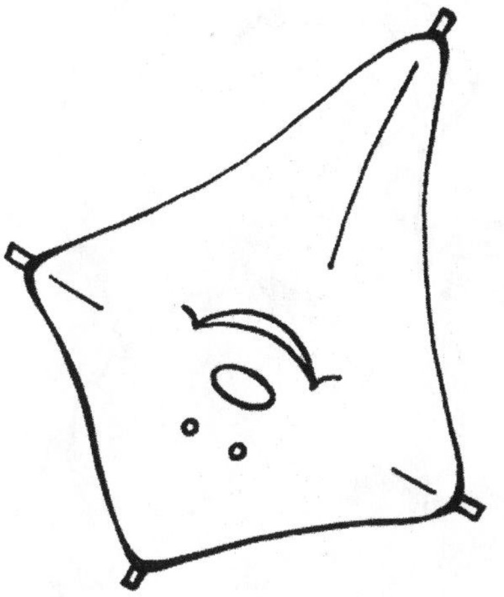

Where is the tail?

It's up in the tree.

The Kite

Where is the string?

I have a tail.

I have a loud roar.

The Lion

I have a mane.

What am I?

He came for pie.

He came for bread.

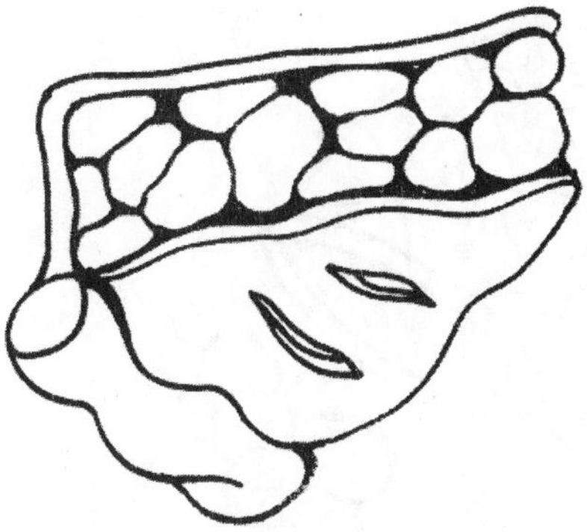

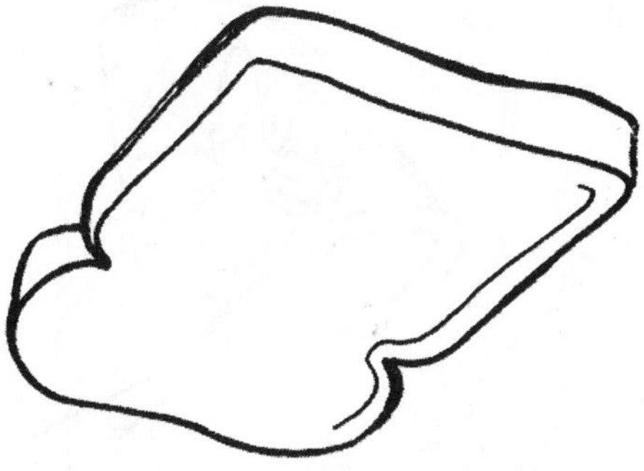

Then he ran away.

The Mouse

He came for cheese.

Dragonflies are in my net.

Fireflies are in my net.

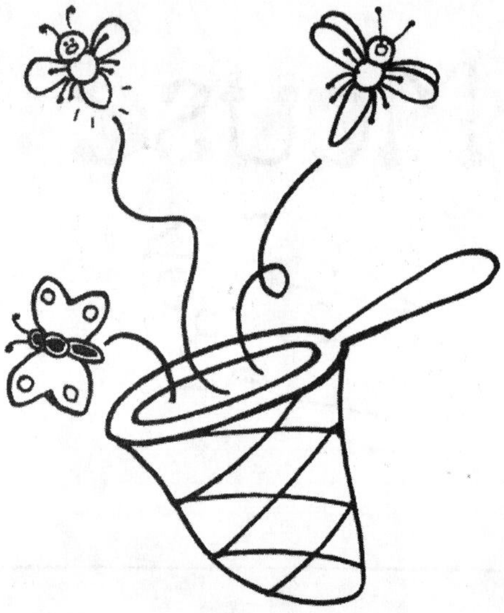

Out they all go.

In My Net

____

Butterflies are in my net.

Wiggle, jiggle, wiggle,

eight arms that jiggle.

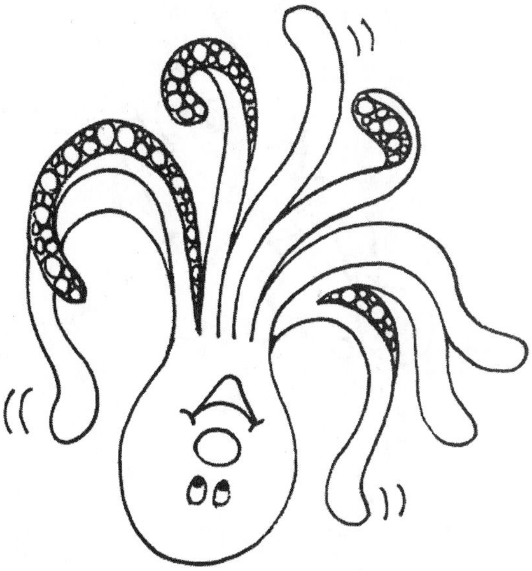

Octopuses

octopuses make me giggle.

Wiggle, wiggle, wiggle,

Pigs

Pigs making popcorn,

pigs in the pool,

pigs playing Ping-Pong—

pigs are so cool!

Quail

There is one daddy quail.

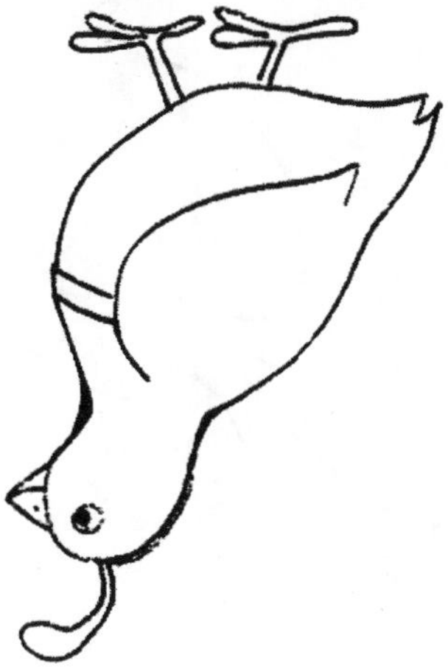

There is one mommy quail.

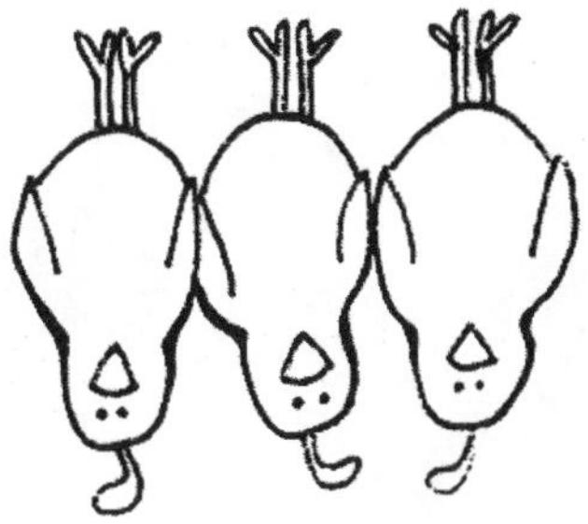

There are three baby quail.

They are on the trail.

His tail is very white.

His ears are very long.

The Rabbit

His eyes are very pink.

See him hop out of sight.

What if the sun shines?

What if the bees buzz?

It is daytime.

The Sun

What if the birds sing?

Trees

There are red apples.

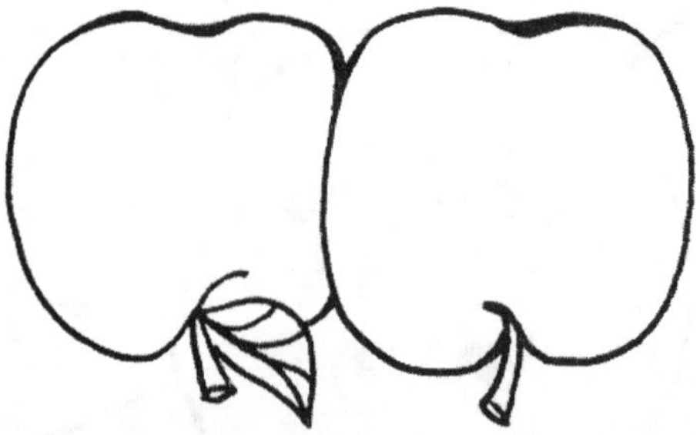

There are green apples.

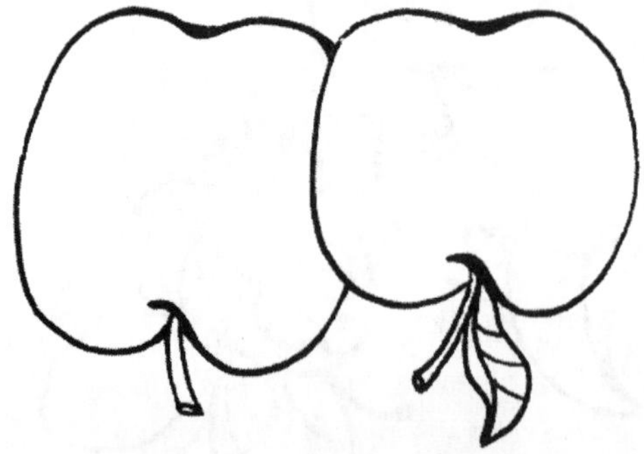

There are yellow apples.

They are in the trees.

I put on my hat.

I put on my coat.

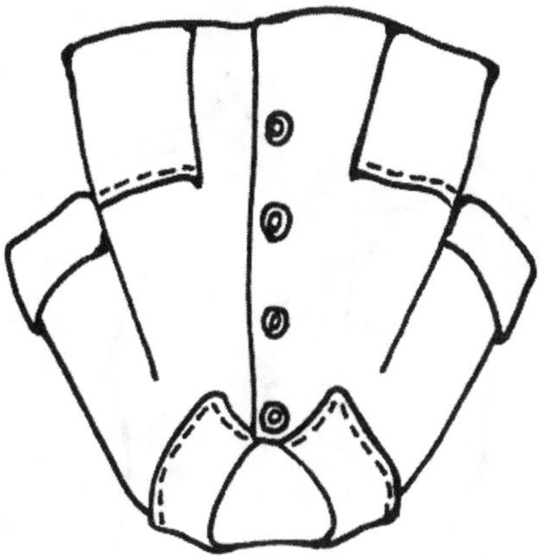

And I carry my umbrella.

Umbrella

I put on my boots.

My vest is red.

His vest is green.

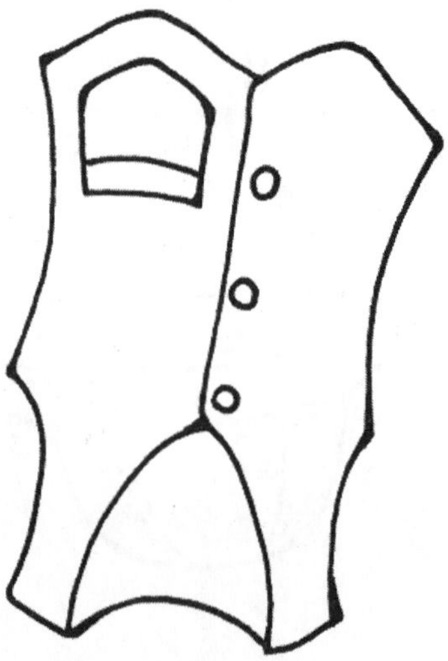

Vests

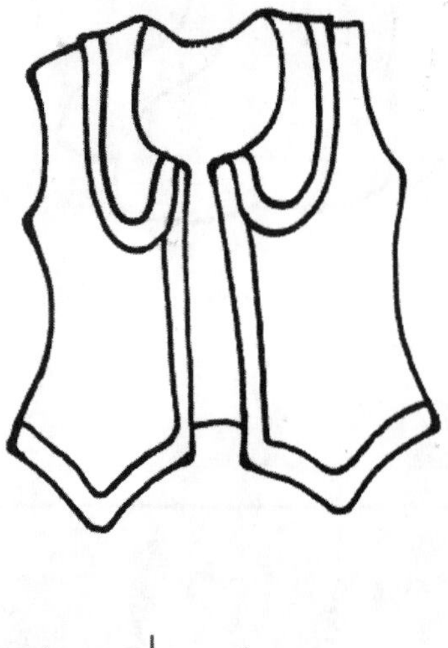

What color is your vest?

Her vest is blue.

Who has eight long legs?

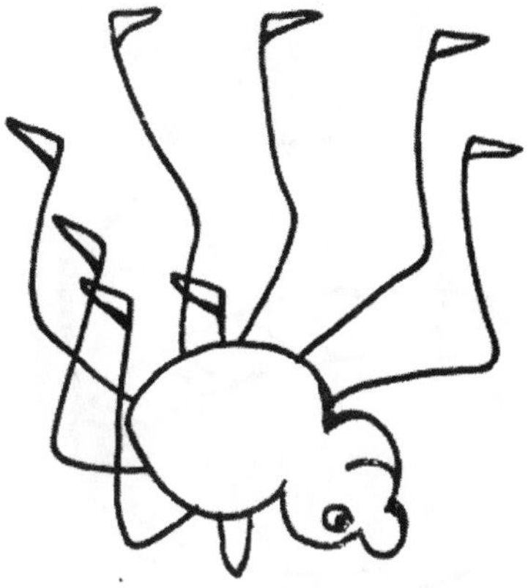

Who can make a web?

Look! It's a spider.

On a Web

Who spins with silk thread?

You can't play in a hatbox.

You can't play in a gift box.

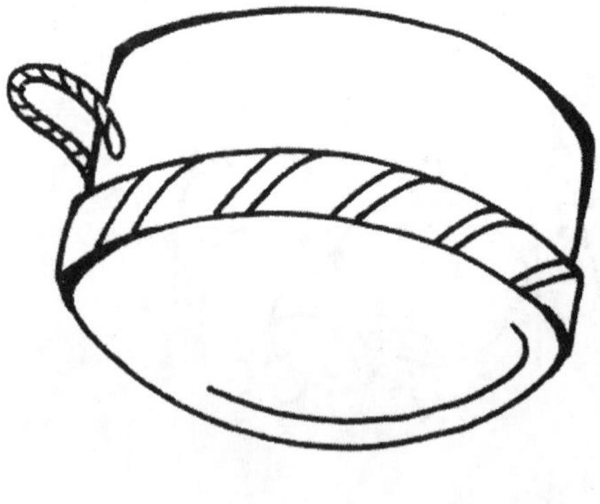

Boxes

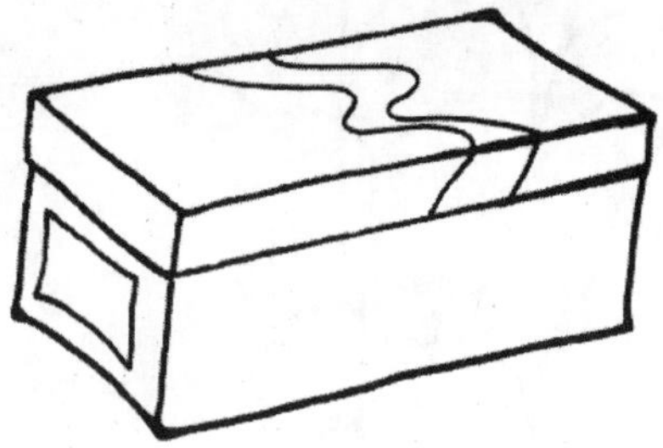

____

You can't play in a shoe box.

But you can play in a sandbox.

and two sleepy yaks

two sad yaks,

make too many yaks.

Yaks

Two happy yaks,

At the Zoo

You will see a zebra.

You will see them at the zoo.

You will see a monkey.

You will see a tiger.

ABC Rhyme with Me: A–Z Pocket Chart Poetry Activities, Poem Cards, and Student-Made Books

Section 6 is divided into three parts:

- Pocket Chart Poetry Activities
- Poem Cards (one for each letter of the alphabet)
- Student-Made Books (one for each letter of the alphabet)

The poems are designed to provide maximum student appeal, incorporating rich language, rhyme, and meter. You may choose to rewrite these poems on sentence strips and use them in a poetry center with a pocket chart, or simply duplicate them and place them in a book format for each student.

Pocket Chart Poetry: Fast and Fun Activities

The use of poetry in the classroom has many educational benefits, including the ease with which you can integrate it into the daily routine of your balanced literacy program. Note the skills each activity teaches.

TRACKING: Thematic pointers can seem magical to students, and the use of these pointers makes tracking print a special, highly anticipated privilege. During a whole-class activity, invite different students to use your special classroom pointer to track the print as the class recites the poem or rhyme.

COUNT WORDS: Give each child a Ziploc bag filled with edible manipulatives (e.g., Goldfish crackers, Cheerios, etc.). Write each student's name in permanent marker on her/his own bag or on an adhesive label so s/he can reuse it throughout the year. Students should take out one manipulative for each word the class reads. Remember to say the words slowly. When you have finished, have students count the manipulatives to determine how many words were in the poem or rhyme. Students will love eating the contents of their baggies once they've finished with this exercise. (**Adaptation:** Invite individual students to use the special pointer to count the words in the pocket chart. Ask the rest of the class to clap and count along.)

CHORAL-READ: Divide students into different groups (by boy/girl, left-handed/right-handed, row, table). Ask each group to choral-read by whispering or using a loud monster voice, or maybe even a speedy "rabbit talk" or slow "turtle talk." Perhaps they would like to sing like an opera star or read with a southern or British accent. Students this age love to be goofy while they're learning!

RECOGNITION: Have the children use Wikki Stix, dry-erase markers, or a pointer to find and show recognition of:

- a particular letter of the alphabet, a capital letter, a lowercase letter
- the letter that makes a chosen phonetic sound
- a particular punctuation mark (What is its job?)

CONCEPT INTEGRATION: Choose poetry that emphasizes cross-curricular concepts such as number words, color words, or science vocabulary.

WORD MATCHING: Copy key words or adhere pictures onto sentence strip cards. Have your students match each word or picture card to the words in the poem.

WORD ORDER: Take the words or sentences off the pocket chart and mix them up. See if the students can put them back in the correct order.

KINESTHETIC LEARNING: Create body movements to go along with a poem or rhyme. Teach these movements, and invite students to "act out" the rhyme or poem. Consider buying or making props to accompany the dramatization.

RHYME: Have students point out the rhyming words in the poem. Put the words up on a whiteboard. Ask the children to share other words that have the same rhyme. List the words after the initial rhyming words and discuss the rhyme pattern.

Example: Jack and Jill went up the hill.

Rhyming Words

Jill *hill* *Bill* *will* *still* *gill* *drill* *spill* *mill* *chill* *thrill*

Questions to Consider

- In what way are these words similar?
- How are they different?
- Can you find a word that begins with a digraph?
- Can you find the common word family?
- Do all the words have the same number of letters? Count and see. Sort and graph.
- Do these words use a short or long vowel sound?

Put these words on flash cards using onset and rime. Blend and segment the words verbally.

COVER THE WORD: After having placed the poem on sentence strips and into a pocket chart, use a piece of cardboard to cover one of the words in the pocket chart. It is best to cover a word that the children are less familiar with in order to build vocabulary. See if the children can guess what word is missing. Slowly reveal the letters in the word one at a time as clues.

Little Miss Muffet sat on a

(answer: *tuffet*)

Ask the students what they think the missing word could be and write their responses on the chalkboard or chart paper: *chair, stool, couch, log,* etc.

Reveal a clue:

Little Miss Muffet sat on a t

What can it be? It begins with /t/. Erase the responses that are no longer appropriate. Ask the students for more responses and write the new responses on the board or chart paper: *table, tail, trunk, trash can, tool bench, trampoline,* etc.

Continue on until the word is guessed and/or uncovered: *tuffet.*

HELPFUL HINTS: Try placing a sheet of acetate or clear laminate over poems in a big book or on a chart. Use dry-erase markers for letter/word play.

Sample Exercises:

- Place a red circle around a capital letter.
- Place a green line underneath each rhyming word.
- Place a purple triangle around the punctuation mark that denotes excitement.
- Place a yellow rectangle around the punctuation mark that denotes a question.

- Find and circle all of the capital and lowercase letter *Mm*'s.

If you find yourself in a time crunch trying to complete all your language arts tasks, try using these activities as a sponge, transitional activity, or dismissal tool.

Poem Cards

Pages 139–164 provide a poetry card for each letter of the alphabet. Follow the reading and discussion of each poem by having your class create a student-made and class books (see page 165).

A Is for Ants

When the ants came to the picnic,
It wasn't very fun.
They ate up all the hot dogs
And munched on every bun.

They got into the salad,
The chips, and chocolate cake.
They even got into my pants.
What next, for goodness' sake!

Bb Is for Bats

Bats are bashful.
Bats are shy.
They wait for dark
To go outside.

Above the trees
They flutter so high,
Then swoop down low
From the sky.

Through the starry
Night they glide,
Then back to the cave
To rest and hide.

Is for Cat

Chasing shadows,
Chasing string,
Cat, you are
A wonderful thing.
How you strut
When you walk about.
How you meow
When you want out.
Then you curl
Up on my lap
And purr, purr, purr
While you nap, nap, nap.

Dd Is for Dogs

Dogs bark;
They howl and moan.
They roll in dirt
And chew a bone.
They lick your face
And scratch their fleas.
Then they go running
Wherever they please!

Ee Is for Eggs

Eggs are excellent.
Eggs are exciting.
Eating eggs
Is most delighting.
Boiled, scrambled,
Deviled, and fried,
Poached, souffléed,
And even dyed.

Is for Frogs

Frogs can swim
With grace and ease,
Dipping and diving
As they please.
But when they are
Upon the land,
They leap about
As best they can.

Gg Is for Goose

A goose is so loud
And quite often nasty!
His honk is atrocious.
His manners are ghastly!
He'll chase you around
For no reason at all,
With his curled-up tail
And a neck that's too tall!

Hh Is for Hat

I have a hat upon my head,
But I really don't know why.
Does it make me look more charming?
Does it shield sun from my eyes?
Is it there to keep my head warm?
Or to keep the rain at bay?
Is it simply there to rest awhile
So I don't have to put it away?

Is for Igloo

Little igloo of ice and snow,
A cozy place for me to go
To sit around the fire's glow
And talk about the day.

Little igloo in the cold,
I love the stories we are told
Of polar bears fierce and walrus bold,
And seal pups at play.

Is for Jar

This jar is special.
This jar is mine.
I'll fill it up
With what I find.

Maybe a minnow,
Maybe a frog,
Maybe some worms
Or a big polliwog.

I'll scoop them up safely.
I'll watch them, and then,
I'll put them right back
In their homes once again.

Kk Is for Kite

Fly so high, little kite,
Past the trees, then out of sight.
Soar beyond the clouds so high,
Climbing up to touch the sky.

L Is for Lion

Little lion, there is no denying,
You are the king of beasts.
With your wisdom, strength,
and courage,
No other can compete.

You walk about the water hole,
And nap beneath the trees.
You roar when you are angry
And eat whenever you please.

Mm Is for Mouse

A tiny mouse lives in my house;
He steals crumbs and bits of cheese.
I wouldn't mind it near so much
If he would just say please.

He's rather cute and furry,
But he isn't welcome here.
Mom would shoo him with her broom
If she knew a mouse were near.

Nn Is for Net

I caught a butterfly in my net,
But she fluttered frantically.
So I let her out
and watched her go,
Then she glided back to me.

She perched upon my shoulder,
And my arm she tiptoed down.
She sat upon my finger,
Then left without a sound.

O Is for Octopus

Oh, I wish I were an octopus
With eight graceful arms.
I'd wrap them all around you
And keep you safe from harm.

Pp Is for Pig

I called my little piggy
To feed him a bucket of slop.
He asked me for another,
And still he would not stop.
With a grunt and oink and squeal,
He demanded another meal.
When I told him,
"Not today!"
He packed his bags
And moved away.

Qq Is for Quail

Gentle little valley quail,
In the bushes and on the trail,
Scurrying in the grass and weeds,
Seeking berries, bugs, and seeds.

Rr Is for Rabbit

Hip, hop, hippity hop,
The rabbit is at play.
His ears will flop.
His nose will twitch.
I wish that he would stay.

Hip, hop, hippity hop,
The rabbit has gone away.
Night has come,
And his burrow is warm.
He simply couldn't stay.

Is for Sun

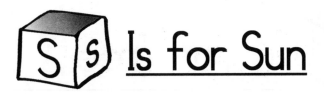

Bright sun, hot sun,
Shine on me today.
Make this morning special,
Watch me while I play.

Bright sun, hot sun,
Chase the clouds away.
Bring along a rainbow
To give me luck today.

Tt Is for Tree

How wonderful to be a tree,
Making shade for you and me,
Holding a hive for the honeybee,
Hiding the nest of a chickadee,
Reaching as high as we can see.
How wonderful to be a tree.

U u Is for Umbrella

Under my umbrella,
Under cloudy skies,
I wish for thunder to rock and roll,
For lightning to strike,
And winds to blow.

I'm wearing my hat,
My boots, and my coat.
Oh, rain, wherever did you go?

Vv Is for Vest

My vest has many colors.
It's soft, woolly, and new.
It's stitched with love and care.
I hope you have one too.

It keeps me snug and warm
When I'm at school or play.
It makes me feel so special,
So I wear it every day!

Ww Is for Web

Spider spins
Her web at night,
With strands so sticky,
fine, and tight.
Her webs aren't meant
for you or me,
But for the bugs
She finds tasty.

Is for Boxes

Big boxes,
Little boxes;
Tall boxes,
Small boxes;
Boxes lined up in a row,
Boxes tied up with a bow.
But what's inside?
I'd like to know!

Is for Yak

There was a yak
Who lived out back.

He grazed all day,
Swishing flies away.

He wore a coat,
All shaggy and brown.
It was so long,
It touched the ground.

Then without a single word,
He left one day to join a herd.

Z Is for Zebra

Is it black on white,
Or white on black?

With four sturdy legs
And a whinny that begs
For carrots crunchy
And apples munchy.

Is it a horse?
It's a zebra, of course.

Student-Made Books

After you and your class have thoroughly read and discussed the preceding poems, have each student make her/his own book. (**Hint:** These books make wonderful end-of-the-year parting gifts for students to take home!) You can also bind together individual student responses to each poem (e.g., When the Ants Came to the Picnic) into one big class book.

The student-made book pages in this section allow students to compose individual responses to the poem cards found on pages 139–164. You will see that each book cover (e.g., When the Ants Came to the Picnic) is followed by the student-made page (e.g., The ants got into _____). On the student-made page students may dictate or write text independently, depending on their ability level, to complete the sentence. In the blank space above the text, students can then draw an object or scene to accompany the sentence. As the teacher, you model a sample page first, then create a graphic organizer to help students generate a variety of ideas that relate to the poem card prompt.

When compiling the student pages of one particular letter into a class book, photocopy the corresponding book cover on construction paper and then write in the authors (e.g., "By Mrs. Vickery's Class" or "By the Students in Room 12"). Next, laminate the cover and a blank piece of matching construction paper (8½" x 11"). Photocopy the corresponding poem and put the book together in the following order:

- laminated cover
- photocopied poem card
- student pages
- laminated back cover

Bind the student-made pages with comb or spiral binding, or simply staple or hole-punch, lacing together with yarn or O-rings. Laminating the covers is optional, but it will lengthen the life of the finished book considerably—especially if the book will be shared with the students' families. Make each finished book part of the class library. Students will love revisiting this collective work!

Below are some possible text responses. Write these ideas on chart paper or on the chalkboard so students can refer back to them.

Eggstraspecial Eggs

I like my eggs scrambled with ketchup.

I like my eggs in a breakfast sandwich.

Octopus Fun

With eight arms I would paint a rainbow.

With eight arms I would color eight pictures at once.

With eight arms I would hug eight people.

Umbrellas

Kaylee has a polka-dot umbrella.

Mark has a broken umbrella.

Heather has a new umbrella.

Zebra Stripes

I saw a zebra with rainbow stripes.

I saw a zebra with a monkey at the zoo.

When the Ants Came to the Picnic

by ______________________________

Name: ______________________________

The ants got into ______________________________________

____

We're Batty About Bats

by --

Name: ______________________________

Bats can ____

____

Copycat

by ____________________

Name: ____________________

My cat and I can ____________________

____

Dog Tales

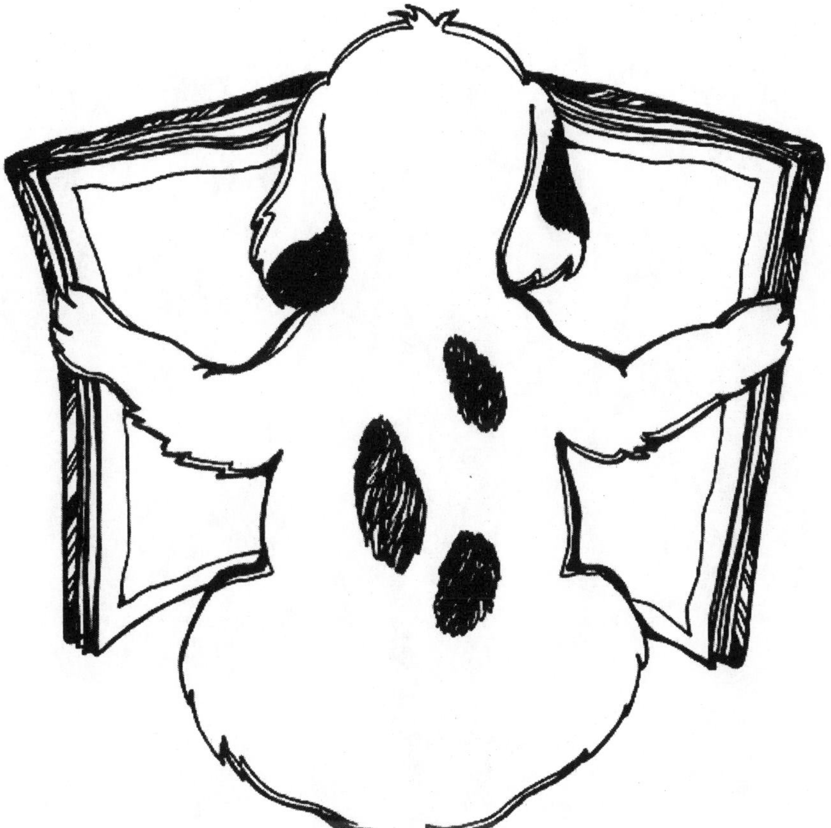

by ____________________

Name: ______________________________

If I were a dog, ____

____

Eggstraspecial Eggs

by ______________________________

Name: ______________________

I like my eggs ______________________

____

Frog Friends

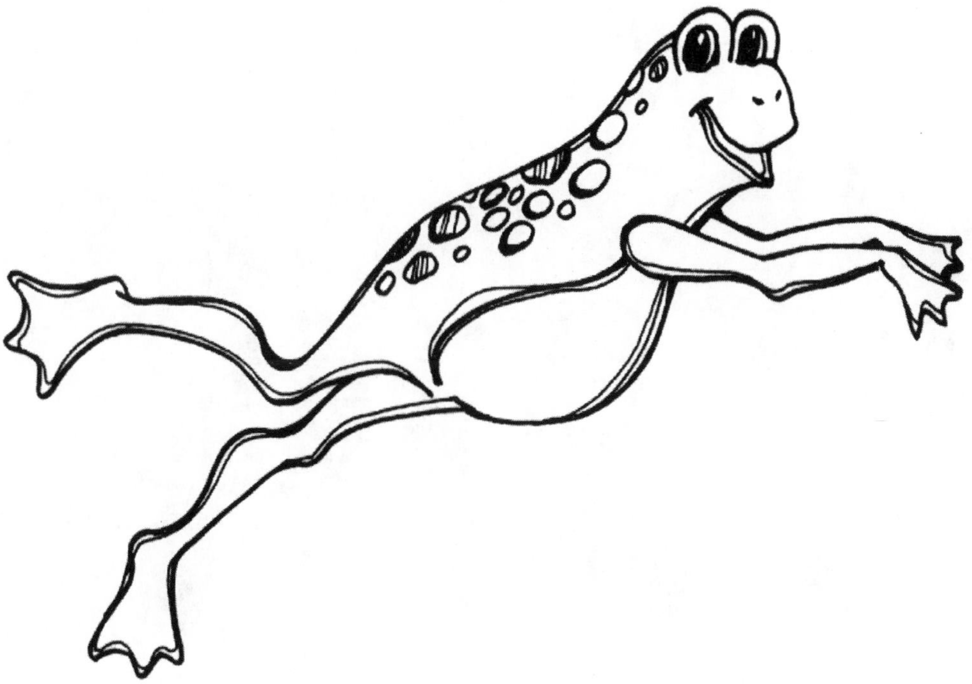

by ______________________________

Name: ______________________________

______________________________ can swim

____

with grace and ease.

Ghastly Manners

by ____

Name: ____________________

My manners are ghastly when ________________

____

A Class Full of Hats

by ____________________

Name: ______________________________

______________________________ has a

______________________________ hat.

Humble Homes

by ____________________

Name: ______________________

I am a ______________________. I live in a

____

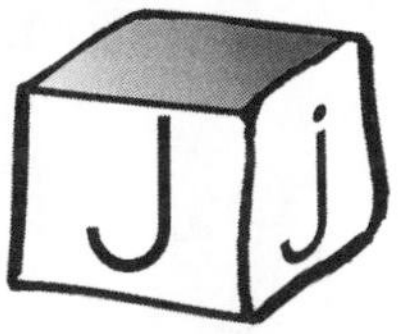

What's in the Jar?

by ____

Name: ______________________________

In my jar there is a ______________________________

____

Kites

by ______________________________

Name: ______________________

I have a ______________________ kite.

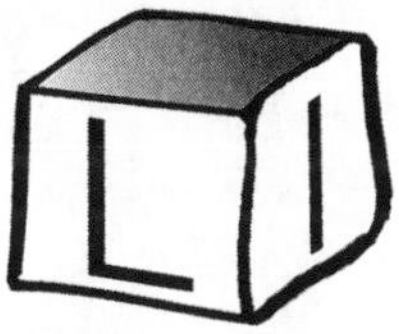

The Lion Is the King of Beasts

by ______________________________

Name: ______________________________

______________________________ is the king of

____

Mouse Meals

by ____

Name: ______________________

The mouse steals ______________________ and

bits of ______________________

What's in the Net?

by --

Name: ______________________________

I caught ______________________________ in my net.

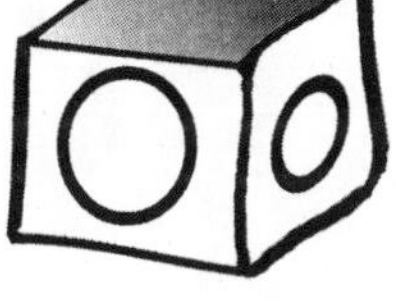

Octopus Fun

by ____

Name: ____________________

With eight arms I would ____________________

____

Pig's Pen

by ____________________

Name: ______________________

Piggy moved to ______________________

____

Along Quail's Trail

by ____________________

Name: ______________________

On the trail I saw ______________________

____

Room _____'s Rabbits

by --

Name: ______________________________

Hip, hop, hippity hop, our rabbits ________________

____

by --

Name: ______________________________

When the sun shines ______________________________

____

Trees Are Terrific

by ____

Name: ______________________________

__________________________ has a _______________________

____ tree.

Umbrellas

by --

Name: ____________________

____________________ has a

____________________ umbrella.

Huggly Snuggly

by ____

Name: ______________________________

I feel snug and warm when ______________________

____

Wonderful Webs

by --

Name: ______________________

A spider caught ______________________ in its web.

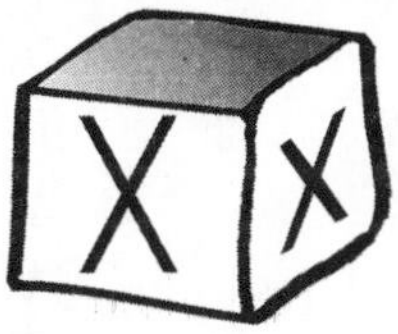

A BoX Full of Surprises

by ______________________________

Name: ______________________________

My box is full of ____

____

A Yak Out Back?

by ____________________

Name: ______________________________

Once there was a ______________________________ who lived out back.

Zebra Stripes

by ____

Name: ______________________________

I saw a zebra with ______________________________

____

Index